19 STARS OF INDIANA

19 Stars of Indiana

Exceptional Hoosier Women

Michael S. Maurer

Foreword by Jo Ann Gora

Published in association with IBJ Media, Indianapolis

Indiana University Press
Bloomington and Indianapolis

This book is a publication of

Indiana University Press
601 North Morton Street
Bloomington, IN 47404-3797 USA

http://iupress.indiana.edu

Telephone orders   800-842-6796
Fax orders   812-855-7931
Orders by e-mail   iuporder@indiana.edu

Published in association with IBJ Media, Indianapolis
41 East Washington Street
Indianapolis, IN 46204

Library of Congress Cataloging-in-Publication Data

Maurer, Michael S.
19 stars of Indiana : exceptional Hoosier women / Michael S. Maurer ; foreword by Jo Ann Gora.
p. cm.
ISBN 978-0-253-35329-0 (cloth : alk. paper) 1. Women—Indiana—Biography. 2. Indiana—Biography. I. Title. II. Title: Nineteen stars of Indiana.
CT3262.I5M38 2009
920.7209772—dc22
2008039581

1 2 3 4 5 14 13 12 11 10 09

For my wife, Janie

CONTENTS

FOREWORD

*O*nly one man in a thousand is a leader of men;
the other 999 follow women.
                                    —*Groucho Marx*

The above quotation is a bit of an overstatement, but then again, Groucho was prone to that. I use it not to stir controversy, but because, in an ironic twist, it quite accurately describes the genesis of *19 Stars of Indiana: Exceptional Hoosier Women*. The book's author, a friend to both Ball State University and myself, succeeded another person who has befriended me and my university, Pat Miller, as Indiana secretary of commerce in 2005. As Mickey describes in the preface, a comment that he made during that transition, and the reaction to the comment, eventually led to him writing this book.

When I was approached about writing this foreword, I immediately began to reflect on the many inspiring Hoosier women I have met and worked with—Pat Miller ranks among them—since I became president at Ball State University in August 2004. Because I was the first permanently appointed female president at one of Indiana's major universities, I am frequently invited to speak to women's professional and leadership groups all over Indiana and am often asked about my own leadership style.

I do talk about that, but I also discuss in some detail my background and how I came to be president at Ball State. And I often ask the group's leaders about their backgrounds, challenges, and triumphs, which creates a dialogue that enriches all of us. What I have found is that we all treasure and learn much from stories—whether our own or those of others. While that sharing is rewarding, it is not necessarily natural or effortless for us. Hoosiers often are reluctant to share those personal stories, and for many of us, especially women, talking about ourselves—how we accomplished our goals, faced our challenges, and overcame obstacles—seems like bragging.

Yet I am convinced that this sharing is how all of us, not only women, develop our own leadership style. We tell our stories; we listen to those of others. We network; we mentor; we seek advice; we gain valuable insights into our own endeavors and our own personalities. We take the wisdom of others and apply it to our own profession, circumstances, and dreams. In doing so, we occasionally find great inspiration.

In reading through this wonderful book, I found that same dynamic at work. Here you will read the personal stories of nineteen Hoosier women who, at first, seem to have little in common other than reaching a certain level of accomplishment. They come from different areas of our state. They represent different facets of society such as business, philanthropy, government, and health care. They had different home lives and received their educations from different schools and universities. But as you move through each chapter, you begin to see those stories connect in certain ways, and those connections lead to valuable insights about ourselves.

Many of these women are not only leaders, but pioneers—the first woman elected Indiana lieutenant governor, the first to establish a Holocaust museum in the state, the first named chief judge of the U.S. District Court in Indiana, the first rabbi to be a mother, and others. Nearly all of these women discuss the importance of integrity in their leadership. These women are motivated to achieve and excel in part because of the sacrifices of those who came before them, particularly family members. And in turn, these women want to pass on what they have learned to the next generation, not in some dictatorial, "Do what I have done" method, but by sharing their stories and offering advice when asked.

All of the women Mickey profiles eventually succeeded because they found their passion and pursued it, even when others may have disapproved. In chapter after chapter of this book, you meet a woman who is not afraid of hard work. You meet someone who believes in the greater good, in benefiting not just herself or the organization she leads, but society at large. And you meet someone who understands that life always brings challenges, and rather than bemoaning that fact, she sees the challenges for the opportunities they also provide.

And here is the best news of all: For nearly twenty years now, more than 50 percent of Indiana's college graduates have been women. I have no doubt that more and more women will move into leadership roles around the state in the twenty-first century. That means that if women such as the nineteen whom Mickey profiles in this book keep sharing their stories, the next generation of female leaders for this state will be even more capable than the extraordinary women described on the following pages. That is something that should make all of us, especially those nineteen women, very proud.

I hope you enjoy reading *19 Stars of Indiana: Exceptional Hoosier Women* as much as I did. Keep sharing your stories!

Jo Ann Gora
President, Ball State University

PREFACE

Pat Miller is a classy dame.

—*Michael S. Maurer,*
Indianapolis Star, *December 13, 2005*

The above response to an *Indianapolis Star* reporter on the occasion of Pat Miller's resignation as Indiana secretary of commerce was meant with all sincerity to be complimentary but was morphed by a *Star* columnist into a slur on the order of Don Imus or Howard Stern.

Pat is a charismatic and capable business leader who founded, along with partner Barbara Baekgaard, Vera Bradley Designs, a meteorically successful ladies' handbag and luggage maker based in Fort Wayne.

At the end of a hard-working year of service to the state, Pat decided to return to the business she loved. We had discussed her impending decision, so I was not surprised when Governor Mitch Daniels announced her resignation. At the same press conference, he appointed me the next secretary of commerce.

Pat Miller did not find my remarks offensive. In fact, she loved the sobriquet. For a long time, she signed her notes and letters to me, simply, "CD." (I hope you enjoy reading her story in this volume.)

From this series of events, an idea emerged. Why not write a book illustrating exactly what I meant when I tagged Pat Miller a "classy dame"? Why not select examples from Indiana's abundant supply of accomplished women and showcase their inspirational achievements?

I enlisted four contributors to help bring this idea to fruition: Greg Andrews, managing editor of the Indianapolis Business Journal, and proficient biographers Nancy Baxter, Dane Starbuck, and Peter Weisz. We were faced with the challenge of establishing a workable standard. How would a woman qualify for inclusion in this book? Financial success? Political office? Celebrity status? Not necessarily. The intangible quality we sought to isolate fell in line with less conventional metrics. We were impressed with the women with panache, the women who made their mark through hard work and ingenuity, and the women who followed their heart while extending a hand to help others.

We finally arrived at a set of criteria. The questions were:

• Is she connected to Indiana? Many well-known women from Jane Pauley to Janet Jackson were born in Indiana, but did not maintain a connection to the state during their careers. We were looking for women who call Indiana home today.

- Is she living? We wished to produce a current collection, not a historical accounting. Figures such as Madame C. J. Walker and Saint Mother Theodore Guerin would otherwise qualify, but they are not profiled here.
- Is her story inspirational?
- Did she make it on her own?
- Did she sacrifice?
- Was she faced with tough choices?
- Does she demonstrate character and class?

We sifted through hundreds of names, many highly qualified, including a number of suggestions from men who nominated their mothers. (My mother deserves her own chapter in this book but for the obvious charge of nepotism that would be lodged.) There is no scarcity of qualified women in Indiana. This book presents only a representative sample, not a comprehensive list. The final selection was not easy.

Our search for the most exceptional women in Indiana was made without regard to location within the state. It's no surprise, however, that Indiana yielded great profiles throughout, as illustrated by the map on page xvi.

Many of the women profiled have lived heart-pounding lives. Each has a unique story. Yet, in spite of the wide diversity, there are common threads:

- Almost half the women benefited from at least one parent who was a professional educator, perhaps further confirmation that preschool education is important to achieving success.
- In these pages, you will find a rabbi, a born-again Christian, and an agnostic who comments on the absurdity of organized religion, but, regardless of specific beliefs, almost all the women professed a deep spirituality.
- Finally, all fully embraced opportunities, regardless of the difficulty. As Sylvia McNair says in her profile, "Take the leap and the net will appear."

I hope readers of this volume will be inspired by these special lives and "take the leap."

ACKNOWLEDGMENTS

Writing is by nature a solitary endeavor. Perhaps that is one of the reasons I enjoy it. The creation of this book, however, was a team effort.

I am extremely grateful for the hard work of this team, particularly the bright and creative writers who contributed chapters. Dane Starbuck (Barker, DeCoudreaux, and Fitzgerald), Peter Weisz (Rivenbark, Owen, and Miller), Greg Andrews (DeHaan, Pescovitz, and Sasso), and Nancy Baxter (Skillman) are talented practitioners whose keen insight is evidenced throughout their work.

I am in debt to Janet Rabinowitch, director of Indiana University Press, who acted as my sponsoring editor. It is an honor to be among the extraordinary titles published by Indiana University Press and I am truly appreciative.

Thanks to copyeditors Andrea Davis, associate editor at the *Indianapolis Business Journal*, and Miki Bird, managing editor of Indiana University Press. Andrea provided many hours of assistance converting the drafts into readable text. Miki refined and polished the manuscript, adding life to the text. I appreciate their patience and careful attention to detail.

Completing the production team are general advisor Ann Finch and design and production experts at the *Indianapolis Business Journal* Jo Hohlbein, creative director, and Pat Keiffner, director of IBJ Custom Publishing, and, at Indiana University Press, Bernadette Zoss, production director. Jo was also responsible for the artwork on the jacket and throughout the book. Pat and Bernie collaborated to guide this volume through the layout and printing processes. Thank you all.

Many thanks to the people who helped facilitate interviews and fact-checked manuscripts, especially Chris Murphy (Raclin), Janet Jarriel (McNair and Brown), and Kathy Pierle (Noël).

A note of appreciation goes to Alvin H. Rosenfeld, director of the Institute of Jewish Culture and the Arts, Borns Jewish Studies Program, at Indiana University, and Holocaust expert, for vetting the chapter on Eva Mozes Kor.

I am indebted to Robin Jerstad and Rich Clark, both professional photographers, for their brilliant work on many of the photographs appearing in this book.

I gratefully acknowledge the valuable research, insightful observations, and cheerful support of my executive assistant, Susan Roederer.

Thank you, Janie Maurer, my wife, who is always my collaborator.

Finally, an extraordinary debt of gratitude is owed to the nineteen remarkable Hoosier women whose private lives are probed in this volume. Their collaboration was essential to the success of the project. Their stories are inspirational and their impact on all of us will be felt for many years.

WOMEN PROFILED

Sarah Evans Barker *(Indianapolis)*: Judge of the U.S. District Court of the Southern District of Indiana

Mary Bolk *(Indianapolis)*: Nurse; medical administrator; Lt. Colonel, U.S. Army Reserve

Angela M. Brown *(Indianapolis)*: Soprano, Metropolitan Opera

Alecia A. DeCoudreaux *(Indianapolis)*: Vice President and General Counsel, Lilly USA; President of Wellesley College Board of Trustees

Christel DeHaan *(Indianapolis)*: Former owner of Resort Condominiums International; philanthropist; founder of Christel House International

Nancy Shepherd Fitzgerald *(Indianapolis)*: Golf champion; founder of Anchors Away Inc. and The Indiana Family Institute

Eva Mozes Kor *(Terre Haute)*: Founder of CANDLES Holocaust Museum

Jeanette Lee *(Mooresville)*: International billiards champion

Sylvia McNair *(Bloomington)*: Faculty, IU Jacobs School of Music; former opera singer; musical theater and cabaret performer

Patricia R. Miller *(Fort Wayne)*: Co-founder of Vera Bradley Designs; former Indiana Secretary of Commerce

Nancy Noël *(Indianapolis)*: Internationally renowned artist and author

Mercy Okanemeh Obeime *(Indianapolis)*: Director of St. Francis Neighborhood Health Center; founder of Mercy Foundation; physician

Jane Blaffer Owen *(New Harmony)*: Philanthropist; historic landmarks preservationist

Ora Hirsch Pescovitz *(Indianapolis)*: President and CEO, Riley Hospital for Children; Executive Associate Dean for Research, IU School of Medicine; Interim Vice President for Research Affairs, Indiana University

Ernestine Raclin *(South Bend)*: Former chair of the board of 1st Source Bank; community leader; philanthropist in arts and education

Sharon Rivenbark *(Nashville)*: Founder of For Bare Feet

Sandy Eisenberg Sasso *(Indianapolis)*: Rabbi of Congregation Beth-El Zedeck; first woman ordained by the Reconstructionist Rabbinical College; children's book author

Becky Skillman *(Bedford)*: Lt. Governor of Indiana; former member of the Indiana Senate

Carolyn Y. Woo *(South Bend)*: Dean of Mendoza College of Business and Professor of Entrepreneurial Studies at University of Notre Dame

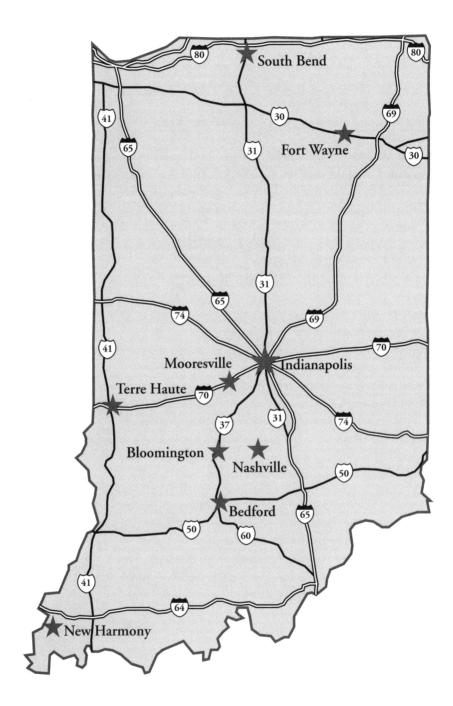

19 Stars of Indiana

Eva Mozes Kor

An Indomitable Survivor

*I*n January 1945, on the heels of the Nazi rout by allied forces, Russian soldiers found Romanian Jewish twin girls, not quite 11 years old, among the ruins of the Auschwitz death camp and transported them to a monastery in nearby Katowice. Nuns escorted them to a clean room—a stark contrast to the utter filth of the concentration camp. The children, whose mother in better times dressed them in identical outfits, were still dressed alike—in rags and swarming with lice. The twins, who had been subjected to cruel experimentation by the "Angel of Death," Josef Mengele, gazed in disbelief at the two beds with white sheets and the toys set out neatly on the table. Eva stared at her clean sheet for a long time before ripping it off the bed and then immediately collapsed on the bare mattress. When she awoke from a fitful sleep, she placed the toys in a corner, remarking to her sister Miriam, "I don't play with toys." Eva was no longer a child.

★ ★ ★

Born on January 31, 1934, Eva and Miriam lived with their parents and two older sisters, Edit and Aliz, in the Romanian village of Portz—population about a hundred. Their father, Alexander, a religious Jew, was a farmer and landowner who married the beautiful Jaffa Hersh from the nearby village of Hida. Alexander's father, who had emigrated from Russia, had developed a fermentation recipe for superior wine. Some of

the local Romanians were barons involved in wine-making, and he traded his expertise for a percentage of the wine-making profits, then used the money to purchase land. After a number of years, the family farm stretched as far as the eye could see. Alexander was next to the youngest in his large family, but he eventually owned all the land, because as his siblings left, he bought them out one by one. The spacious home had a tile roof—an upgrade from most villagers' straw roofs—and a long, open porch to which many rooms in the house had direct access. Eva's father had thirteen brothers and sisters and countless cousins, many of whom often visited the farm. It was a happy time.

Eva was almost 6 when World War II began in Europe. Soon after, the Hungarian fascists occupied her village and her childhood took an abrupt turn. Upon entering first grade, she learned that children can be mean and, if they're given the opportunity to hurt others and are then rewarded for the misdeed, they can become adept at it. She and her twin sister were teased, beaten up, and spit upon—and there was nothing they could do. They were caught in the maelstrom of anti-Semitism.

In April 1944, Eva and her family were removed from their village at gunpoint by Hungarian gendarmes and taken with the few belongings they could carry to a large field surrounded by a barbed-wire fence. This was a ghetto of about seven thousand Jews who were brought in from the surrounding area. They lived in tents made of sheets. There was only one building, the commandant's headquarters, to which every head of a family was taken for a day of interrogation. Eva's father, among the last to be interrogated, was returned to the family on a stretcher, bleeding from whip marks. All of his fingernails and toenails had been burned with candles in an effort to determine where he had hidden his gold and silver.

A few days later, the family was loaded onto a cattle car with countless others. Positioned in a booth between the cars, a guard with a machine gun announced that he would shoot anyone attempting to escape. Once a cattle car was loaded beyond capacity, the doors were closed and a metal bar was placed across the handle, firmly hooking it into position. There was no way a person from inside could force it open.

It was dark and unbearably hot inside the cattle car. The train moved fast, traveling for days and stopping only to refuel. On those occasions, the occupants of the cattle car would ask for water. The guard in the booth would reply, "Five gold watches." The adults gathered the watches they had hidden and passed them to the guard, who then threw a small bucket of water through the window. No matter how Eva held her cup, it was impossible for the water to reach her through the crush of the other occupants. There was no food.

When the train stopped at the end of the third day, the prisoners again asked for water. This time the response was in German. Hungarian guards had been exchanged for Germans when the train entered German-occupied Poland. In Portz during the earlier years of occupation, the Jews had heard rumors of Jews being taken by Germans and killed. All hope vanished with the sound of those German guards—people began to cry and pray. Everyone understood their plight. There was no escape. When the train rolled on, people sat in the darkness of the cattle car in terror-induced silence. Several hours later, the train stopped. Pleas for water were met with no response. Alexander Mozes gathered his family and said, "Children, I do not know where we are, I don't know what will happen, but if any of you survive this terrible wrong, I want you to go to Palestine. I believe that Jews can live in Palestine in peace and freedom." He began to pray. Eva was angry, resenting that her father's way of dealing with the catastrophe was to pray to God.

The train arrived at daybreak at the Auschwitz II death camp known as Birkenau and, as the cattle car doors slid open, Eva heard Germans yelling, "Schnell! Schnell! Raus!" ("Fast! Fast! Out!"). Thousands of people poured out all along the train tracks. Within ten minutes her father and two older sisters had disappeared. She never saw them again. Eva was overcome with the smell that permeated the camp, which she later learned was scorched flesh and burned hair. Huge barbed-wire fences loomed as Germans yelled orders. Here and there she could hear dogs barking and families screaming as they were ripped apart.

While their mother held on to Eva and Miriam, who were dressed alike, an SS guard spotted them. He ran back and forth, yelling "Zwillinge!" ("Twins!"). Guards were under orders from camp doctor Josef Mengele to search for twins to be used for medical experiments. The SS guard demanded from her mother if they were twins, and she answered yes. Immediately, another SS guard pulled their mother down the platform as the twins were yanked in the opposite direction. Eva looked back and saw her mother's arms stretched out in despair as she was dragged away. That was the last time Eva saw her. She and Miriam would spend more than nine months in Auschwitz.

The twins were segregated and placed in a huge room. Their clothes were taken away and they sat naked on bleachers for the better part of that first day. Late that afternoon, the processing began. Their hair was cut short and their clothes were returned with a huge red cross painted on the back. Then they were lined up for registration. When it was Eva's turn, she resisted. Four people restrained her while a pen-like device with a metal tip was heated over an open lamp flame. When it was red hot, a woman inmate dipped it into ink and burned into Eva's left arm "A-7063." Miriam became A-7064.

After registration, the twins were marched to their barracks. From the back of the barracks, the children could see flames glowing bright red. Smoke covered the entire camp and the smell was terrible. When Eva asked what was burning, she was told, "Jews." That night, Eva went to sleep on a bottom bunk bed that was covered with a thin straw mattress and a filthy blanket. She noticed large dark objects moving on the floor. She jumped up, screaming "mice." A child on the top bunk replied, "Those are not mice. They are rats and you might as well get used to them because they are everywhere." Eva couldn't sleep, so she and Miriam went to the barracks latrine, where they saw the corpses of three children on the floor. Eva made a silent pledge that she would do anything within her power to ensure that she and her sister would not meet the same end. She never let fear or doubt deter her from that vow.

The next morning, Mengele entered the barracks with his entourage.

During roll call, the dead bodies from the latrine were taken out to the front of the barracks. They had to be counted. Later in the morning, female prisoners loaded the corpses into carts and took them to the crematorium to be burned with those who had been gassed the day before. When Mengele saw the bodies, he began to scream, "Why did you allow these children to die?" Eva later realized he was upset because every time a child in the barracks of twins died, he lost two guinea pigs. If one twin died during an experiment, the control twin was killed with an injection into the heart and comparative autopsies were performed.

After a breakfast consisting of only a brownish cup of liquid, the experiments began. The experiments were conducted ostensibly under the supervision of the Kaiser Wilhelm Institute for Genetic Research, but most historians regard Mengele's treatment of the twins as little more than an exercise in cruelty. The experiments contributed nothing to the advancement of scientific knowledge. Every Monday, Wednesday, and Friday, the twins walked an hour to an experimental lab in the main Auschwitz camp, where they were placed naked in a room with twenty to thirty other pairs of twins for six to eight hours while every part of their body was measured, recorded on charts, and compared to their twin sibling. Every movement was noted. Although these experiments were not dangerous, they were demeaning. Eva thought she was treated like a living piece of meat.

On Tuesdays, Thursdays, and Saturdays, the twins went to the blood lab, where they sat fully dressed on benches. Technicians tied down both of Eva's arms and drained blood from her left arm until she fainted. At the same time, they gave her at least five injections in her right arm. After one of those injections she became ill with an extremely high fever and her legs and arms became swollen, with painful red splotches. Although it was July and hot outside, she trembled with chills. Eva tried to mask her reaction because she was aware that those taken to the hospital did not return. On Eva's next visit to the lab, they measured her fever and took her to the hospital. She knew she was in jeopardy.

The hospital was a camp in itself, filled with the living dead. Eva was placed in a small room with other twins who told her that they didn't receive any food, water, or medication, since "people are brought here to die." The following morning, Mengele entered with four other doctors, looked at her chart and laughed sarcastically, saying, "Too bad, she's so young, she only has two weeks to live." Eva refused to die. She made a second silent pledge that she would prove Mengele wrong. She would survive and be reunited with Miriam. For the following two weeks, she was between life and death. Somehow she discovered that there was a water faucet at the opposite end of the barracks. She crawled on the bare floor to the water when she could no longer walk. She faded in and out of consciousness but even in her semiconscious state told herself, "I must survive."

Once in a while, she saw the silhouette of a woman who entered at night and placed a piece of bread on her bed. The woman had told Miriam that her sister was continuously fainting because of her sickness and the lack of food, so Miriam saved her bread for her sister for an entire week. It was extraordinary for anyone, particularly a child of 10, to refrain from eating a whole week's ration in order to prevent someone else from starving.

In June 1944, allied bombing of the area began and by August the bombs rained down more often. Although no bombs fell on the camp, the experiments waned as the barrage intensified. The bombing eventually slowed to four times a day, and then ceased altogether by November. In January 1945, the Nazis abandoned the camp. One morning after they had fled, Eva sneaked into the kitchen and grabbed several loaves of bread. From the kitchen, she heard the sound of a vehicle. When she went outside to investigate, four SS troopers jumped off a jeep, pulled their machine guns and began to spray bullets in every direction. A soldier pointed the barrel of a machine gun at Eva's head. She awakened later among bodies lying on the ground. She reached out and touched one of the bodies. It was ice cold. She realized that she had fainted before the bullets hit her.

In the middle of that night, she was again awakened, this time by explosions. In an effort to destroy evidence, the Nazis were blowing up the gas chambers, the crematoriums, and all related buildings—including her barracks, which was on fire. She and Miriam went outside, where the SS told them to march. The whole world was aflame. Anyone who could not keep pace was shot on the spot—of 8,200 people who marched out of Birkenau on the night of January 17, only 7,000 survived. As soon as the group completed the four kilometers to the main camp at Auschwitz, the Nazis disappeared as if the earth had swallowed them up. But the deed had been done. More than one million Jews had gone up the chimneys of the Auschwitz death camp.

There was no water to drink at the camp, so Eva went to the river, broke through the ice and lowered a container by a string into the water. When she looked across the riverbank, she saw a girl about her age dressed in beautiful clothing, her braided hair tied with a ribbon. This was Eva's first realization that not all children were living her nightmare; the child looked back at Eva, who was just bones held together by skin and rags.

A few days later during a gusty snowstorm, Eva saw four or five snow-covered figures moving toward her; they were smiling and they didn't look like Nazis. In fact, they were part of the advancing Soviet Army, a force allied with the United States. The girls ran up to them and were given chocolate and cookies and hugs. This was the first human kindness that Eva had experienced in a very long time. Her vow that she and Miriam would survive hell became a reality. They felt a tremendous sense of triumph—they had endured unbelievable evil. They were alive and they were free. But life would never again be the same.

While in Auschwitz, Eva had a naïve image of returning with Miriam to their home and rejoining their relatives. That dream had to be postponed for nine months as the twins were shuttled to three different refugee camps in the Soviet Union. When they finally made it back to their village of Portz in October 1945, the twins learned that no one in their immediate family had survived. The gas chambers had claimed almost all of their extended family, about 117 people in all. The family's house was ransacked, their belongings stolen by the neighbors, and the property neglected. On the once magnificent porch stood her mother's dog, Lilly, a red dachshund. In the house, all that was left were three crumbled pictures on one of the bedroom floors. Title to all of the real estate was confiscated during the Holocaust, never to be returned.

Eva and Miriam found an aunt in Portz who had miraculously survived, and they lived with her for five years. Romania was under oppressive Communist rule and there was tremendous poverty at that time. Sometimes Eva would stand in line for ten hours for a loaf of bread.

In 1946, Eva traveled to nearby Cluj to attend the first Holocaust memorial service. The rabbi at the service asked anyone who had any soap from the camps to bring it to be buried because it was made of human fat. Eva was shocked to hear that the few bars she had hoarded were made out of her people. She subsequently had frequent nightmares, hearing the voices of her parents yelling at her, "Why are you washing with us?" These persisted until she left Romania.

The twins immigrated to Israel in June 1950, when they were 16. As they left Romania, they were allowed only what was on their backs. Their aunt put three dresses on each girl and a winter coat despite the season. On the ship *Constanza*—built for a thousand passengers—three thousand refugees left Romania. It was to be the last ship to depart Romania for Israel for four years. The ship landed in Haifa in the morning. As the sun rose over the mountains, the passengers burst into song. Upon arrival in Israel, the girls were taken to Magdiel, a youth village near Kfar Saba that housed children ages 7 to 18 from thirty-five countries. Eva learned to say "I love you" in ten languages. On the first night, they danced Israeli dances. That also was the first time since she was 6 that Eva could remember sleeping through the night without fearing that somebody would harm her because of her religion.

At age 18, after two years in the village, the twins were drafted into the Israeli army. Eva stayed in the army for eight years, rising to the rank of sergeant major. When she was 26, she met Michael (Mickey) Kor, another Holocaust survivor, who was visiting his brother in Israel. He had been liberated in the concentration camp in Buchenwald by American colonel Andrew Nehf, who resided in Terre Haute, Indiana. Kor planned to immigrate to Indiana.

Eva did not speak English. Mickey did not speak Hebrew. They carried dictionaries. He would say something and she would look it up. Communication was a challenge, but in spite of that they married on April 27, 1960.

After waiting two and a half months for a visa, Eva Kor arrived in Terre Haute on June 19, 1960, to join her husband. She has lived there ever since. After a year or two of living with this cantankerous young woman, Mickey said, "I thought you were very quiet." Eva replied, "I couldn't speak the language." He did not marry a quiet woman. The marriage has succeeded nevertheless.

Eva Kor became a U.S. citizen in 1965, after the birth of their son Alex in 1961 and daughter Rina in 1963. Immediately upon gaining citizenship, she joined the League of Women Voters and later participated in Bobby Kennedy's presidential campaign. In 1977, Kor began a career in real estate sales, which she continues. In 1990, she received a bachelor's degree in vocational and technical education from Indiana State University.

Kor returned to Auschwitz in 1984 as an American citizen. She had always wondered what had become of the other twins who survived, and so she tracked down 122 of them—six of whom joined her on that trip. Many survivors could not afford the trip and some said they couldn't endure the cold. Others were not emotionally prepared to return. But for Kor, it was a liberating experience. She could go up to the barbed-wire fence, touch it, and no one was going to kill her. She could walk into the camp and walk out. She was exhilarated to know she was free to do as she chose. Victory. Still, she felt that there was one thing left to do: Forgive.

For many years Kor hated the Nazis and the Germans. She hated the whole world. Hatred controlled her and defined her being—until she decided to forgive. According to Kor, most people come to the idea of forgiveness from a religious perspective. In her case, forgiveness has nothing to do with religion nor has it anything to do with the perpetrator. She believes that by forgiving, she can free herself and regain control over her life. "In 1945, I was freed physically. In 1995, I was freed emotionally. Forgiveness is for you, not for anyone else. Getting even has never healed a single person," she says. Kor has delivered her message of forgiveness in innumerable lectures to schools, synagogues, civic groups, and other organizations. She wants to introduce her idea of forgiveness to teachers, so students can be taught a skill that will help them lead a good life. "We teach them reading, writing, arithmetic, and how to cross the street, but we don't teach them how to heal themselves from the little hurts," she said. "Forgiveness is free, it works, and has no side effects. I call it miracle medicine. Forgive your worst enemy. It will heal your soul. It will set you free."

Kor's concept of forgiveness has raised the ire of many in the diminishing community of Holocaust survivors. Some claim that implicit in forgiveness is the concept of pardon and acceptance. Her position is controversial.

In April 1995, Kor established in Terre Haute the only Holocaust museum in Indiana, CANDLES (Children of Auschwitz, Nazi Deadly Lab Experiments Survivors) in honor of her sister Miriam, who had died two years earlier from cancer of the bladder, undoubtedly a consequence of an injection of one of Mengele's cocktails. Kor had been able to return her sister's kindness before her death, donating her left kidney to her twin in 1987, when Miriam's kidneys failed as a result of Mengele's experiments.

In 2003, the CANDLES museum was burned to the ground, a despicable act initiated by an arsonist, suspected of being a white supremacist. The day after the fire, Kor received a call from then-governor Joe Kernan, who asked what he could do. Kor had an answer: "I would like a half million dollars to help rebuild the museum." Not able to do that, he helped her reinstate her property insurance—a task accomplished that same day. Mickey and Eva Kor were invited to the State of the State

Address in 2004 as Kernan's special guests. The CANDLES museum, newly rebuilt, reopened the following year as evidence of her indefatigable spirit.

Kor is busy. In addition to her real estate career, she continues to speak publicly about her experiences and the lessons to be learned from them. Kor advises, "Never give up. You can survive anything. To be in this mixed-up world, one has to be tough." Her reach has been wide. Kor has appeared on the *Oprah Winfrey Show*, *Good Morning America*, *60 Minutes*, and *Larry King Live*. She was named newswoman of the year by the Israeli press in 1985, received the Martin Luther King, Jr. Spirit of Justice Award in 2004, and won the Daughters of the American Revolution Americanism Award later that year.

Kor is a living testimony to the strength of an indomitable will, and a role model for all who wish to forgive. As his last act as governor in 2005, Kernan awarded the Sagamore of the Wabash—at the time, Indiana's highest honor—to Eva Mozes Kor, a little girl from the Nazi extermination camps who would not die.

Christel DeHaan

The Entrepreneurial Philanthropist

Entrepreneur Christel DeHaan considers herself fortunate. Some of the world's neediest children feel the same way, thanks to DeHaan's decision to devote much of her wealth to giving them a better life. After selling Resort Condominiums International (RCI) for $825 million in 1996, the Indianapolis resident set up a worldwide philanthropic organization, Christel House International, which runs four schools serving impoverished children in foreign countries. She has poured more than $78 million of her own money into the not-for-profit so far, and expects to spend tens of millions more.

The generosity overwhelms the students, who know her as Miss Christel. Even though many have next to nothing, they shower her with gifts—chocolates, crocheted handkerchiefs, and other items—during her annual weeklong stay at each school. "Going across the schoolyard, there are hundreds of hugs, hundreds of kisses," DeHaan said. "Little notes are passed on. It's their way of saying, 'Thank you.'"

Those are heartwarming moments for DeHaan, whose own childhood in bombed-out post–World War II Germany taught her something about hardship. She hopes that by giving the children a boost, they'll raise themselves up and achieve their potential, just as she has.

★ ★ ★

DeHaan never fathomed she would have the resources now at her disposal to improve the world. Before she and her then-husband, Jon DeHaan,

started RCI in their Indianapolis home in 1974, Christel worked as an administrative assistant at an RCA record-manufacturing plant in Indianapolis. At the start, their two sons and neighborhood children helped with mailings and membership kits.

Resort Condominiums International was a pioneer in the now-booming business of time-share exchanges—allowing people who own one week at a ski resort condo, for instance, to trade it for a week in the Caribbean. Christel received control of the company in 1989 in one of the highest-profile divorce battles in Indiana history. The victory ended her two-year banishment from the business. She returned to RCI as CEO, and more than doubled its size in just seven years. By the time the business was sold, it had annual revenue of $345 million. The 1996 sale to New Jersey–based HFS Inc. made DeHaan one of the richest women in America.

The sale also was a bonanza for the company's 4,300 employees. In addition to handing out large sums to her senior management team, DeHaan gave surprise checks to rank-and-file workers based on longevity in the company, not on position in the corporate hierarchy. Between the two groups, payments totaled $125 million.

While the sale of RCI garnered headlines in business publications across the nation, what happened next was equally extraordinary. Rather than rest on her past successes and enjoy her fortune, DeHaan launched Christel House International, reaching out to poor children in some of the nations where RCI had enjoyed business success. It was her way of giving back.

It wasn't a career path DeHaan had scripted. After completing the sale of RCI and retiring from the business, then 54-year-old DeHaan had planned to downshift. She and four of her former RCI colleagues intended to run her family foundation, which she'd started a few years earlier to support arts and education causes. "I thought, 'We are going to update its protocols and structures, and so on and so forth, and life will be glorious,'" DeHaan says. "'We'll go home at 3 o'clock in the afternoon. We'll have a nice little office downtown, and life will be great.'"

What changed the course of her life was a phone call she received in 1998 from a former RCI colleague in Mexico. He asked if she would be willing to provide financial support for two orphanages there. She said she'd consider it, but wanted to visit the orphanages first. What DeHaan saw on that initial trip to Mexico City overwhelmed her.

"Mother Ines—a Franciscan nun who runs both orphanages—had a rather well-meaning idea to remove the older boys from 'the sins of the city,'" DeHaan recalled in an interview a few months after the visit. "They were housed in a place that I refer to as 'the wilderness' two hours outside Mexico City. The boys lived there with a caregiver; they walked eight miles to school, there was no electricity because of a broken generator, and the water came from a cistern."

DeHaan quickly surmised that another plate of food or another piece of clothing would not solve these boys' long-term problems. "You stand there and you fast-forward five years," DeHaan said. "Boy marries poor girl from village, has a family and cycle starts all over."

As she rode back to Mexico City on a Volkswagen bus, DeHaan pondered this parable from the twelfth-century philosopher Maimonides: "Give a man a fish and you feed him for a day. Teach a man to fish and you feed him for a lifetime." That moment has guided DeHaan's life since. She opened her first Christel House in Mexico City in the fall of 1998. In 2001 and 2002, she added schools in Bangalore, India; Cape Town, South Africa; and Caracas, Venezuela. Christel House International also operates a charter school in Indianapolis and a tutoring and after-school program in Serbia for refugee children.

Christel House International's foreign outposts are more than schools. Most of the students come from slums, barrios, or informal settlements. DeHaan's philanthropy provides them with school supplies, uniforms, and shoes, as well as annual medical and dental checkups, vision screenings, and immunizations. They also receive two meals a day—often their only source of nutrition. DeHaan isn't satisfied giving the children a safe haven. She expects them to succeed in the classroom. Students receive rigorous academic instruction, especially in language arts, reading, and math. English-language fluency and computer skills receive extra attention, because they give graduates an edge in the job market.

It's an overwhelming and expensive undertaking. Christel House International has an annual budget of $14 million. DeHaan has funded the bulk of it herself, though now that her schools are showing successes, she's ratcheting up outside fundraising efforts. She continues to run her family foundation but now directs most of her charitable giving to Christel House International. The children have benefited immeasurably. But DeHaan said she feels enriched, too.

"I am by nature an entrepreneur. I need to build and create, and I needed to have more than the family foundation," DeHaan said. "I always had wanted to do something that would make a huge difference in somebody's life, but I could never figure out what that was. But when I went to Mexico, I got the epiphany."

Today, DeHaan is the picture of poise and sophistication. She has perfectly coifed hair and a passion for high culture, including music and art. But appearances belie the realities of her rough-and-tumble childhood. Christel and her older sister, Evelin, grew up in the German city of Nordlingen in Bavaria in the aftermath of World War II. Her father, Adolf Stark, a German soldier, died weeks before the war's end. Her stepfather, Wilhelm Riedel, died when she was 16.

"I grew up in very, very difficult times," DeHaan said in a 2001 interview. But she had the advantage of a strong-willed mother, Anna—a loving disciplinarian. She recalls her mother saying, "I will show you how to survive."

"We are in the main a composite of our genetic makeup and our environment," DeHaan said. "My mother instilled my values in me."

Though DeHaan's family was solidly middle class—the household had fineries such as china, silver, and crystal—after the war money was in short supply, and food sometimes was scarce. But her mother was enterprising. The family would pick leftover potatoes from farm fields, and would stretch scrambled eggs by adding water and flour. Her mother augmented the family's income by owning and running a mangling shop, where linens were pressed. The family matriarch also loved the arts and played several instruments. Christel and Evelin took accordion and recorder lessons, and both girls were encouraged to listen to opera on the family's portable record player on many Sunday afternoons.

After graduating from a Catholic academy in 1958 at age 16, DeHaan spent a year as a nanny in England, then returned home to begin exploring job options. Family friends suggested she take advantage of her ability to speak English and pursue a position with the U.S. Armed Forces. In 1959, she landed a job as the youngest administrative assistant and translator at Grafenwöhr, a U.S. Army base in West Germany.

There, she met the man who would become her first husband, Ralph Cobb, an Indianapolis native who was serving as a medic in the army. When his tour of duty ended in 1962, they settled in Indianapolis. Christel and Ralph had two sons, Keith and Tim. To help make ends meet when the children were young, Christel started her first business—an ironing and typing service—which she ran from their home. The couple divorced in 1971. "It was a traumatic moment in my life, but sometimes people grow apart," DeHaan said. Soon, she enrolled at Indiana Central University, now called the University of Indianapolis, to pursue a bachelor's degree.

Christel met Jon DeHaan through a blind date arranged by one of her classmates, whose husband worked with DeHaan at an Indianapolis architectural and engineering firm. Jon was a creative, entrepreneurial type who had been involved with several business ventures. At the time, Christel was working as the administrative assistant to the RCA plant's head of quality control.

Jon and Christel married in 1973; the same year, they started research and development work on RCI. They launched it a year later. Jon had hit upon the idea for the company while doing a project for the American Resort Development Association. The resort industry needed a big boost. The nation was mired in recession, interest rates and inflation were in the stratosphere, and an OPEC-imposed embargo had caused oil prices to quadruple. The resort association had enjoyed success with an exchange program for recreational vehicle owners. Jon thought that applying the concept of exchange to resort condos would increase demand for the badly overbuilt industry. "I saw a lot of waste in the whole-ownership of condominiums," he said in a 1975 interview.

He noted that most condo owners were leaving their units empty about two-thirds of the time. There was a need, Jon believed, for people to be able to swap their empty condo units during the year for units they would be more likely to use. "The seed of our success," he said, "is that we identified that unserved exchange niche."

Back then, resort developers typically sold 100 percent of each condo to a single buyer. RCI initially helped orchestrate trades between those buyers. The fledgling industry took off as developers began selling not just to one buyer, but to as many as fifty-two buyers, with each owning the unit one week or several weeks out of the year, guaranteeing them their own vacation hideaway. RCI didn't own or develop the condos, but it played a critical role in the growth of the industry because purchasers viewed the exchange feature as a critical part of the buying decision. To make exchanges, time-share owners paid annual membership fees, plus a fee for each exchange.

The company had a synergistic relationship with developers, who sold far more units than they would have otherwise. "Part of the brilliance of the RCI model is the resorts became our distribution network," Christel said. "We helped the resorts sell their inventory. In so doing, we also received our customer." RCI closed its first year with a mere $16,000 in revenue. She and Jon kept track of exchanges on index cards. But it wasn't a mom-and-pop business for long. In 1977, RCI installed a Wang computer system, automating its exchanges for the first time. Four years later, it upgraded to a state-of-the-art IBM system.

Automation was crucial because facilitating equitable exchanges was tricky. Rather than making direct exchanges with other owners, members deposited their weeks into the "RCI SpaceBank." That meant they could choose a vacation destination without needing to have an owner in that locale sign up for their unit. The RCI system took into account that certain units were more desirable than others based on several factors, including unit size and season of the year.

By the early 1980s, RCI had rocketed into the ranks of Indiana's fastest-growing companies. In 1985, *Indianapolis Business Journal* recognized the DeHaans' achievements by naming RCI the winner of its annual

Enterprise Award. The vacation resort industry, which once struggled with a semi-sleazy reputation, had arrived—and RCI had played a pivotal role in fueling the growth. When RCI held its sixth annual international conference that year in Orlando, Florida, former U.S. president Gerald Ford was keynote speaker, and three hundred convention delegates from eighteen countries hobnobbed at pool parties.

But behind the scenes, Christel's and Jon's marriage was unraveling. Jon, the majority owner, ousted her from the business in late 1986. The couple sought a divorce the following February. Christel was devastated to be cut off from the company. RCI had become an ever-larger part of her life through the 1980s, as Jon increasingly was hamstrung by serious health problems. He suffered a heart attack in 1979, then had heart bypass surgery in 1984. That was followed by angioplasty procedures in 1985, 1986, and 1987. In the divorce proceedings, Christel testified that Jon was hospitalized thirty-four times in four years and became "very consumed with dying. It was very, very difficult for him to live in such a fearful world, very difficult for me who loves life and embraces life."

Christel had owned just 20 percent of RCI. But during the twenty-seven-month divorce case, Marion County superior court judge Anthony Metz ruled that 20 percent understated her involvement. He valued her stake at 50 percent. "If you really look at all the literature the company put out during the time that both parties were associated with RCI, they kept talking about it in terms of partnership, in terms of the founders, Christel and Jon DeHaan. It wasn't just Jon DeHaan, ever. It seemed to me that both parties were equally necessary in what they did to get the company where it is," Metz wrote.

Christel valued the company at $135 million and sought to be a buyer or a seller at 50 percent of that value. Judge Metz ruled that Christel would be the acquirer—a decision that shocked Jon and his attorneys. They claimed it was the first time that a U.S. court turned over a company primarily owned by one spouse to the other, without giving the majority shareholder the right to buy. "I assumed we'd get control of the company, and we'd have to pay Christel a huge amount of money," Jon said days after the ruling. "Instead, I had one hour to pack up my office and get out of the building."

Earlier, Jon's attorneys had offered a settlement of $11 million, an amount that would have left her set for life. But she was unwilling to accept an offer she deemed unfair and inequitable. "I was told by my then-attorney, 'You better take the offer that's on the table, because you may end up with nothing,'" Christel recalled. "My answer to him was, 'Don't ever ask me to compromise on something I think is the right thing to do, the fair thing to do. If that means I get nothing, so be it.'"

Christel said that she and Jon had a "wonderful complementary relationship" before their marriage fell apart. In the early years, he drove the company's strategy. "I've always said I would not have been able to do RCI on my own. Jon probably could have done RCI on his own, but he probably couldn't have sustained it on his own."

Metz based his ruling on three key issues: the extent to which each participated in the company, the management abilities of each, and the state of Jon DeHaan's health. He ruled that while Jon had had a positive influence on the business, he had turned over more responsibilities to vice presidents as his health declined. While both were capable of running RCI, Metz said, "the evidence seems to indicate [that Christel] is the better manager."

She returned to RCI one day after the ruling. After shaking up the executive offices with the dismissal of senior executives, DeHaan plunged into expanding the company's international reach and adding services for members and time-share developers. She acquired a travel agency in 1990, a property-management company in 1991, a computer software company in 1995, and the time-share industry's dominant research company a year later. Her management style isn't for the timid. She doled out lucrative compensation packages for top talent. But she also was demanding, showing little patience for colleagues ill-prepared for meetings.

DeHaan waged a no-holds-barred battle for market share with the No. 2 exchange company, Miami-based Interval International, which started two years after RCI. After Interval International began advertising its first conference in Asia to woo developers, DeHaan promptly scheduled RCI's first Asian conference two weeks earlier. She repeated the stunt after Interval scheduled a conference in Spain that year.

As RCI thrived, suitors began knocking. For years, DeHaan wasn't interested. "I had a great love of the company, and I felt I wanted to take it to several of the next plateaus," she said. But after she met Henry Silverman, the CEO of New Jersey–based HFS, for lunch in the summer of 1996, she began giving the idea of selling the company serious consideration. Publicly traded HFS was in a host of businesses—including hotels and rental cars—that complemented RCI's, opening up new growth opportunities.

DeHaan made quite an impression on Silverman during their get-together. The HFS leader, a demographics nut, got caught up in DeHaan's discussion of how baby boomer trends would boost the time-share industry, according to a *Business Week* profile of Silverman. Before lunch ended, Silverman told the magazine, "I convinced myself, and had her half-convinced, that we should buy the company." He added: "This is not a good negotiating tactic—drooling and groveling—but I did both of those."

In the sale, DeHaan received $550 million in cash, $75 million in stock, plus the potential to earn another $200 million if RCI hit certain performance thresholds. It later met those goals, entitling her to the full payout. "It was really a risk assessment," she said of the sale. "I thought, 'Two years from now, who knows where the stock market is?' It could have been greater; it could have been less. The fact of the matter is, I know Henry Silverman and HFS got a good deal when they bought RCI. This was not a decrepit, declining company. I was happy with what I got. I didn't have to squeeze every last penny out."

DeHaan's decision to share her windfall with all of her RCI colleagues is legendary. When *Indianapolis Business Journal* heard what DeHaan had done, a company spokeswoman vehemently tried to dissuade the newspaper from reporting it. "She did this out of the kindness of her heart, not for publicity purposes," the spokeswoman said.

Some workers got wind of the gifts in advance when a grid used to determine the exact amounts of employees' checks had somehow circulated through several departments. "The head of the mail room was approached by a Vietnamese woman who'd been working in the mail room since 1980," a former employee recalled. "She said, 'Is it true? Is it true that my husband

and I will get $14,000?' Her supervisor said, 'No. You and your husband will get $40,000.'" Some lower-level employees received enough to pay off their home mortgages or send children to college. "Astonishing checks were handed out," one employee recalled. "People were just thunderstruck."

DeHaan said giving the money was not a difficult decision. "This was done in recognition of their devotion, and in recognition of my philosophy that when you have, you also share," she said.

DeHaan knew that she didn't want to run someone else's company. So after helping with the transition to new ownership, she walked away from the business she had helped build for more than two decades. The change was a jolt. "The loss I felt was not being able to work with the people who were so dear to me," she said. She also was wrestling with an empty nest. She and Jon's only child together, Kirsten, had just gone off to college.

Within months of the sale's closing, DeHaan was making a splash in philanthropic circles. She and her family foundation gave $3.5 million to local arts organizations, $1.5 million toward construction of the White River Gardens at the Indianapolis Zoo, $1 million to the Eiteljorg Museum of American Indians and Western Art, and $8 million for the Christel DeHaan Fine Arts Center at the University of Indianapolis—a project that combined her two main passions, education and the arts. DeHaan never finished her University of Indianapolis degree, but she is one of the college's biggest champions and has served as chair of its board since 1997.

Though she came to Indianapolis by happenstance, DeHaan has grown passionate about it. "I think Indianapolis is a good place to raise a family, to work, and to start a business," she says. "I have grown to love Indiana. I regard it as my home."

But none of her passions has been as all-consuming as Christel House International. DeHaan serves as CEO of the not-for-profit, which she insists must be run with the same sharp management practices she applied to RCI. Its annual report notes that Christel House International received a perfect four-star rating from Charity Navigator for two consecutive years, in recognition of its efficient and effective management. The report is packed with bar charts showing students' improving achievements.

DeHaan plans to remain CEO for the next several years. The Christel House in Venezuela started with older students than the other schools, and its first graduates are now attending universities or technical schools or doing apprenticeships. She wants to stay at the helm to see them land good jobs and become contributing members of society. At that point, DeHaan, who will be approaching 70, plans to continue as chairwoman but pass the CEO's role to a successor.

It's a very personal crusade for DeHaan, who works with Christel House staff to build relationships with students and parents. During one visit to Mexico City captured by a Forbes reporter, a slight 17-year-old girl, abandoned by her prostitute mother, clung to DeHaan, unwilling to let her leave. DeHaan embraced the child, stroked her hair, and kissed her face. "That's what it's all about," DeHaan later said. "These kids, they are just yearning for love."

DeHaan continues to pump huge sums into the not-for-profit. Though she expects outside donors to pick up more of the slack in the future, she has no plans to halt funding. She intends to leave an endowment that will generate enough income to cover general and administrative expenses as well as operating shortfalls in perpetuity. That will ensure that 100 percent of what other donors give will go directly to helping children. And though DeHaan will leave some of her fortune to her own children and grandchildren, most will go to Christel House International.

Her Christel House support is separate from the more than $50 million she gave through the years to her family foundation and a related charitable fund. The family foundation now donates more than $2 million annually, much of it to arts organizations. "I ended up being an extremely fortunate human being," she said. "I learned a lot, achieved a lot, and then had significant financial resources."

What better way to use it, she says, than to give children a seat at the table of life?

"If I had not sold RCI, who knows what I might have done?" DeHaan says. "It's an academic question. The fact is I did, and I did something with my life that continued to add meaning and purpose. So I feel all right."

Sarah Evans Barker

The Role of a Lifetime

On the morning of November 17, 2000, more than a hundred lawyers from the nation's most prestigious law firms filed into a majestic, marble-adorned courtroom in the U.S. Federal Building in Indianapolis, prepared for battle. Their task: to litigate hundreds of lawsuits arising from alleged defects in Bridgestone/Firestone tires installed on Ford Motor Company's popular Explorer sport utility vehicles. More than 270 deaths and nearly 1,000 injuries were linked to the tires, which ultimately were recalled. On the bench that day was U.S. District Court Judge Sarah Evans Barker, a native Hoosier chosen by her colleagues to supervise one of the largest and most complex pieces of litigation in U.S. history.

Though the cases originated in state and federal courts throughout the country, a panel of federal judges decided to consolidate them into a single venue. Barker was someone "with the ability and temperament to steer this complex litigation on a steady and expeditious course," panel chairman John F. Nangle wrote in his transfer order. She was up to the challenge, despite the sheer volume of cases and the bevy of challenging procedural and legal issues they raised. Mixing her trademark clarity and firmness with a characteristic touch of humor at that first hearing, she put the litigators on notice: "I was thinking of the old Bette Davis line: 'If you want to get something done, give it to a couple of old broads,'" Barker said to the courtroom full of attorneys, referring to herself and U.S.

Magistrate Judge V. Sue Shields, who sat next to her at the bench. "Let me tell you, these old broads are going to get this done!" That they did. The judicial tag-team of Barker and Shields resolved more than eight hundred Bridgestone/Firestone cases between 2000 and 2006, generating praise from both plaintiffs' and defendants' attorneys alike.

★ ★ ★

Nominated by President Ronald Reagan and confirmed by the U.S. Senate in 1984 as the first female federal judge in Indiana, Barker has achieved an extraordinary record on the bench—not bad for a self-described "late bloomer" who didn't contemplate a legal career until she was almost finished with college. "There weren't any other attorneys in the family," she explained. "Along with most other people at that time, my parents didn't know any women lawyers and generally thought that 'nice' people didn't need a lawyer."

Born in 1943 in Mishawaka, Barker was the second of six children in a family that valued education. Her father, James McCall Evans, was an electrical engineer and her mother, also named Sarah, taught fourth grade. They met in their home state of Arkansas in the 1930s, married in 1938—the year after James graduated from Purdue University—and moved to the northwest Indiana town of Mishawaka in 1941, when James began working for the Wheelabrater Company. During his forty-year career there, he earned an MBA from Indiana University's South Bend campus. Teachers weren't required to be college graduates at the time, and Barker's mother had finished just one year of higher education before moving. She kept at it, though, eventually earning a bachelor's degree from Bethel College in Mishawaka—taking one class each semester for twenty years while also raising her family. She later completed a master's degree.

"My parents were strongly committed to education—their children's and their own," Barker says. "They knew it would open up opportunities that would not otherwise be available."

Indeed. Barker's older sister, Margie Miller, is a retired Spanish teacher who has taught at both the high school and collegiate levels. Her younger sister Lora Stout, holds a doctorate in education and is assistant superintendent for curriculum and faculty development for a large school system outside Detroit. One brother, James M. Evans Jr., is a United Methodist minister in northern Indiana. Another, Joseph Evans, is a registered nurse at a hospital near Philadelphia. The baby of the family, Amy Stant, is married and resides in Indianapolis with her husband, John. Both are living with cerebral palsy, something Barker says makes her youngest sister a "very special person" who is an inspiration to others.

As a child, Sarah was a playful tomboy who loved to be outdoors, riding her horse, building a tree house, or assembling a raft to float down the creek near their home. Like many Hoosiers, she shot baskets at the goal affixed to the garage and played with the neighbor kids in their large barns and haylofts. Schoolwork was a lower priority for her, though her parents made sure her grades didn't lag.

"I was not interested in sewing and cooking. . . . I did them, but only so I could also take woodworking and sheep-raising, which were regarded as 'boys' projects," she says. "To this day, I'm not very interested in domestic tasks."

Still, she did learn the value of hard work. As a girl, she made money babysitting and selling raspberries she picked in the family garden. She used her earnings to pay for "extras," including church camp. In high school, she worked at the school bookstore and as a file clerk for a local car dealership, and picked up shifts at a dime store during summers and holidays. During her undergraduate days at Indiana University, she was employed by an accountant during the school year and spent four "glorious" summers as a camp counselor at a private girls' camp on Lake Thompson in Oxford, Maine.

At Mishawaka High School, Barker was student council vice president and president of the Indiana State Y-Teens, an organization affiliated with the YWCA. She was a "respectable alto" in the school choir and had leading roles in school plays and musicals. She played guitar in the jazz band and percussion—drums, cymbals, and the glockenspiel—in the marching band. She was awarded a Good Citizen Award during her senior year and was voted "class clown" by her peers in the Class of 1961.

Barker stayed active after enrolling at Indiana University in the fall. She was elected president of her dorm, Sycamore Hall, and served on the IU Student Foundation board. She also pursued her musical interests as a member of the Singing Hoosiers. And she kept playing—this time as a member of the intramural basketball, baseball, and volleyball teams. "Intercollegiate competitions for women athletes had not been developed at that time," Barker explained, "but our teams won several all-campus tournaments during those years. We were good!"

She balanced a variety of activities and responsibilities successfully during college, preparing herself well for the life she would carve out for herself in later years as a wife, mother, and lawyer. For most of college, she envisioned herself entering one of the traditional career paths for women at the time, such as nursing or teaching. Not many women became doctors or lawyers, but the lucky ones married them—as she would eventually. Barker never considered going to law school until one of her dorm counselors suggested it during her junior year at IU. Once the seed was planted, she figured out a way to make it blossom.

After graduating from IU in the spring of 1965 with a bachelor's degree in social service, Barker earned money for law school by working for a year as a residence hall director at the University of Rhode Island. In fall 1966, she enrolled in the nation's first law school, at the College of William and Mary in Williamsburg, Virginia. She chose the small school because it was so different from the Big Ten university where she had done her undergraduate work. But after her first year there, Barker transferred to American University in Washington, D.C., where she had landed a job with the parole board to pay for her education.

At the start of her final semester of law school, Barker took a position as legislative aide to Congressman Gilbert Gude, who represented Maryland's Eighth Congressional District. After completing law school in 1969, she became a legislative assistant to Senator Charles H. Percy and later served as special counsel to the Senate Government Operations Committee's Permanent Subcommittee on Investigations.

"I loved the energy and fast-paced life of Capitol Hill," Barker recalled.

"Some of the big issues of the day included busing to work towards deseg-regation of the public schools, gun control, environmental regulation, defense spending for controversial weapons systems, and the Vietnam War. Since this was the time shortly after the assassination of Martin Luther King and Robert Kennedy, racial violence also preoccupied the public agenda."

In early 1972, she left the position of special counsel to become Percy's director of research, scheduling, and advance work for his re-election cam-paign. She stayed on board through his victory, then left Washington to become part of another legal movement—marriage. That November, she wed her former high school and college classmate Kenneth Barker, who was practicing law in Indianapolis. They had been friends since their days in Mishawaka and stayed close during their time in Bloomington, but did not develop romantic feelings for one another until years later. Kenneth attended Harvard Law School, then served in the U.S. Army as an officer and attorney until 1970, when he returned to work at the Indianapolis law firm Bose McKinney and Evans. Sarah tapped her government contacts to apply for a position with the U.S. Attorney's Office in Indianapolis.

Although she didn't know it at the time, Barker became the first female assistant U.S. attorney to serve in Indiana when the Honorable Stanley B. Miller hired her in 1972. She was far from a figurehead, prosecuting numerous cases over the next several years—everything from tax evasion to illegal drug trafficking. Barker enjoyed the excitement of trial work and proved to be "pretty good" at it, she says. When the Honorable James B. Young replaced Miller as United States Attorney for the Southern District of Indiana in 1976, he promoted Barker to first assistant U.S. attorney— essentially his chief of staff and right-hand woman. The years Barker spent prosecuting cases for the government gave her valuable experiences from which she later would draw when appointed a federal judge.

But first came a stint in the private sector. After President Jimmy Carter's election in 1976, he nominated fellow Democrat Virginia Dill McCarty to be U.S. Attorney for the Southern District of Indiana, effec-tively overhauling the Indianapolis office. When Barker left, she joined

Bose McKinney and Evans—from which her husband had recently resigned—as an associate specializing in litigation. Her experience put her on the fast track there, and Barker became a partner three years later.

In 1980, politics again brought about change when Ronald Reagan was elected president. After taking office in 1981, he appointed Barker to replace McCarty as U.S. Attorney and she returned to the Indianapolis office as the district's top federal prosecutor. She was honored to be select-ed—and to lead the charge on cases that would remain part of Indiana's judicial lore. High-profile cases included the conviction of Phillip Gutman, the former president pro tem of the Indiana Senate who was found guilty of accepting bribes from the Indiana Railroad Association; the conviction of so-called "Speedway Bomber" Brett Kimberlin, whose actions terrorized an Indianapolis community; and the convictions of sev-eral residents who were running a multimillion-dollar cocaine operation, one of the largest drug rings in the state's history.

When U.S. District Judge Cale J. Holder died suddenly in 1984, Reagan appointed Barker to fill the vacancy. She was just 40 years old. In speaking publicly the first time about her selection, Barker fought back tears. She announced to well-wishers that she supposed "people would have to get accustomed to a federal judge who sometimes gets weepy." More than twenty years later, she has developed a commanding presence on the bench—without abandoning that softer side.

Barker was among those in the Indianapolis community who grieved when federal probation officer Tom Gahl was fatally shot while on duty in 1986, leaving behind his wife and two young sons, ages 8 and 4. Because she had worked closely with Gahl—both during her tenure as U.S. Attorney and on the bench—Barker reached out to his widow, Nancy. For more than twenty years, they have spent the anniversary of his death together, doing something special to remember him. The first year, they returned to the scene of the shooting and left a rose before traveling to Methodist Hospital to rock babies in the intensive care nursery. In other years, the women have served food at a soup kitchen, delivered hot meals to shut-ins, and planted flowers. When Nancy Gahl was diagnosed with cancer in 1995, Barker arrived early at her doorstep to deliver a bouquet of lilacs from her home garden. Out of horrific tragedy, a special friendship developed and still flourishes.

In her more than twenty years on the federal bench, Barker has ruled on a number of high-profile cases involving complex legal issues. She mandated an end to overcrowding at the Marion County Jail, then levied fines when the sheriff's department did not comply. She ordered the seizure of the Indianapolis Baptist Temple after church leaders failed to pay $6 million in federal taxes and refused to turn the property over to the government. She also has ruled on numerous constitutional claims, including Indiana's controversial voter-identification law, which requires voters to present government-issued ID in order to vote—one of a handful of cases she's been involved in that have ended up before the U.S. Supreme Court. The high court affirmed her ruling in April 2008.

Just ten years into her term, Barker was named the district's chief judge, taking on additional administrative duties and adding another first to her resume. She is proud of breaking ground for other women, but at the same time Barker is deeply aware of the responsibility to perform well so others can follow in her footsteps.

In addition to all her professional accomplishments, Barker is known for her sense of humor. In 2000, she received the Man for All Seasons Award from the Indianapolis St. Thomas More Society, an organization of Catholic lawyers and judges. Barker, a member of the United Methodist Church, took the designation in good stride. "Is this the St. Thomas More Society's salute to menopause?" she remarked during her acceptance speech. "Have I worn my black robe so long that it has caused people to forget who and what is underneath it? Or maybe my selection . . . is the lawyers' way of telling me I need a refresher course at charm school."

In May 2007, Barker delivered a commencement address at the Garrett-Evangelical Theological Seminary north of Chicago, where she also received her ninth honorary doctorate. The seminary summarized her address in a news release, noting that "Barker kept a nearly full house . . . laughing with an Indiana barn full of jokes and stories that would make

Jay Leno proud." Perhaps as a result of her quick wit, she is in demand as a public speaker around the state of Indiana.

Although Barker has a lifetime appointment to the bench, the law is not her entire life. She is also a wife, mother, and grandmother; she's a daughter, sister, aunt, and friend—all roles she holds dear. The Barkers have three grown children and two grandchildren. The only other lawyer in the family, her husband, has retired. "I couldn't have done what I have in my life and career without the support of Ken," Barker says. "He's the one who has held the center of the family steady. His willingness to take on many of the family and house responsibilities has freed me up to put in the long hours that are required of my position. I greatly admire his many strengths and gifts, but I am especially grateful for his willingness to be there for all of us."

The couple lives in rural southern Johnson County, adding two hours of drive time to Barker's already-long days. She uses the time to decompress. During her daily drives, she enjoys listening to books on tape when she's not reveling in the silence of the solitary trips. In what little free time she has, she dabbles in photography, enjoys attending concerts and plays, and takes pleasure in books. Barker devotes much of her outside time to organizations she strongly believes in. She has a long history of varied service on judicial, advisory, and not-for-profit boards, serving as a director of the Indiana Historical Society, the Conner Prairie Foundation, various educational institutions, and Clarian Health Partners Inc., where she chairs the Values, Ethics, Social Responsibility and Pastoral Services Committee. Barker also has maintained lifelong, active involvement in her church, continuing the pattern that her parents set for her and her siblings when they were children.

"I've always tried to stay involved in the outside community as much as time would allow," she says. "I believe it has made me a better lawyer and judge. It's important to me to problem-solve in a way that requires me to figure out in advance what the best direction may be instead of doing it always in retrospective, as you do as a judge."

In 2007, Barker undertook a two-year term as president of the Federal

Judges Association, a voluntary organization with about nine hundred members across the country. The group focuses its efforts on issues of judicial independence, salary fairness issues, and employment benefits.

"Judges can't issue press releases to defend their judgments or generate support of their decision," Barker says. "The ability of the courts to render fair and impartial judgments in the cases assigned to them is key to the rule of law. Unfortunately there are many factors that threaten that independence. As the third branch of government, judges' rulings must be followed, whether agreed with or not."

Barker reports that she is often approached by young people who express an interest in following in her footsteps, particularly in seeking to balance the demands of a profession as well as a family. Her advice: "Find somebody to make the journey with you who is just as committed to doing both as you are. You have to expect to be torn in the process of trying to do both and doing them both well, because, whatever you are doing, at one point in time part of you will always be thinking that 'I should be doing the other.'"

Barker's personal goals are as simple as they are ambitious. "I want to be a good grandmother, a good wife, a good daughter, a good judge, a good friend. None of us is just one person; we all have many roles and there is only so much time," she says.

On being the first woman federal judge in Indiana, Barker reflects, "When young lawyers, especially women, share with me that they themselves want to be a judge someday and they ask me about the process of getting to be one, I tell them, 'The only straight line is when you look back. There is a lot of luck involved and the stars have to align right. You have to prepare, of course, but in addition you have to have enough chutzpah to grab for the brass ring when it comes around. And if it doesn't come your way, you must not regard that necessarily as a set back; you just go a different direction.'"

The citizens of Indiana are fortunate that the stars have aligned for Sarah Evans Barker. No one is more surprised or grateful than she that her life worked out the way it has.

Sylvia McNair

Taking the Leap

*I*n May 2006, Sylvia McNair sat with her doctor at an urgent care center in New Jersey. McNair, a highly acclaimed soprano, had shared her extraordinary and diverse musical talents in concert halls, theaters, and cabarets throughout America and in every major international performance venue. She had collaborated with the renowned musicians of the day and had sung with the Vienna Philharmonic for Pope John Paul II at the Vatican. She was held in high esteem in recognition of the quality of her work. She had earned rave reviews. That day, however, the news was not so good. The doctor was gentle but direct. Although a mammogram performed six months earlier was clear, a new test had detected invasive ductile carcinoma. McNair had an aggressive breast cancer that already had advanced to Stage III. "I hope I am wrong, but you may not celebrate Christmas," her physician said, advising her to see an oncologist for chemotherapy and perhaps radiation. "It will be rough. You need to make some plans." McNair was undaunted. "This won't defeat me," she told him. "I should make plans. I will plan a dinner party for the night before my first session of chemo."

★ ★ ★

Born June 23, 1956, McNair was an only child who benefited from the focused energy of her talented and devoted parents. Her mother,

Marilou McNair, an elementary and junior high school music teacher, put her on the piano bench when she was 3 years old. She began violin lessons at the age of 7. The McNairs lived in Mansfield, Ohio, a city of approximately fifty thousand about an hour southwest of Cleveland, where the family attended concerts. Her dream as a child was to play the violin in the Cleveland Orchestra. In a sense, she accomplished that goal. Although she never sat in the string section of the Cleveland Orchestra, she sang with the orchestra many times and once, in the course of a performance, incorporated a violin solo.

McNair's father, George, an employee at appliance maker Westinghouse Electric Corporation, also played the violin and piano. He could be moved to tears by a Tchaikovsky symphony or Brahms violin concerto, McNair says. Her father had an artistic soul while her mother had the discipline and teaching credentials. They all sang. With marvelous DNA and an encouraging environment, it is little wonder McNair had magnificent raw musical talent that, when developed, would delight audiences throughout the world.

Young Sylvia was her father's "only son." She was immersed in sports before she learned to read. She and her father attended football, basketball, and baseball games and rooted for their favorite Ohio teams. "I can throw a softball with the best of them," McNair brags. In high school, she excelled in track. Her long-jump record at Lexington High School stood for seventeen years. At 5'9", she has maintained the figure and grace of an athlete for more than three decades, perhaps because she is an award-winning ballroom dancer proficient in swing, fox trot, and cha-cha.

Fulfilling her father's wishes, McNair enrolled at Wheaton College in Wheaton, Illinois, as a music major with a concentration in violin. Wheaton, a small, church-affiliated liberal arts school, has a solid music department, but it is hardly comparable to the finer schools of music. "He really wanted me to go to Wheaton because his family could not afford to send him there. I loved to make my dad happy," she says.

Most summers during high school and college were spent at jazz and chamber music clinics and music camps, honing McNair's violin and piano skills. Her original goal was to be an orchestral violinist, an easier career path than the concert-violinist route because there are never fewer than thirty violins in a major symphony orchestra.

Then McNair had a conversation with her violin teacher, Howard Beebe of Ohio University, which eventually changed her professional aspirations. "I think you should take voice lessons," Beebe told her. "Learning to sing will improve your violin skills. It will make your violin sing. It's in the breathing." McNair understood. Good music requires proper breathing technique, much like yoga. According to McNair, "Music comes from a very deep place in your heart and soul and it requires breath to support that. It's like football players who take ballet—a different discipline that supports your primary goal." Halfway through college, in the midst of a voice lesson, McNair realized she was having more fun singing than practicing the violin. With the cautious support of her parents, she made a pleasure-driven choice to set down her bow and concentrate on her voice. Today, she plays the violin professionally only as a part of her one-woman show and even then she has, for the most part, transitioned from classical music to bluegrass and show tunes. She loves to perform "The Great American Songbook"—songs by the likes of George Gershwin, Harold Arlen, Cole Porter, Richard Rodgers, and Stephen Sondheim.

In looking to further her education after graduating from Wheaton, McNair applied to only two schools: Indiana University and The Juilliard School. She was not interested in studying anywhere but at the best of the best. "I wanted to shoot for the top and deal with whatever happened," she said. Juilliard declined her application, making the choice an easy one. McNair enrolled in the Indiana University School of Music in August 1978.

She arrived in Bloomington, Indiana, with little self-assurance. IU music students are some of the most capable young performers in the world. Nevertheless, McNair excelled there. During graduate school, she performed a number of operatic lead roles on campus. Her voice, characterized as "lyric soprano," was well-suited for Handel, Bach, and Mozart. She made her professional debut with the Indianapolis Symphony Orchestra in 1979, during her second year in graduate school, when she was paid $400 to sing a Bach cantata. "It was like winning the lottery," McNair said. "It was huge."

Her luck continued in September 1980 when she returned to IU for the fall semester. Atlanta Symphony Orchestra music director Robert Shaw had arrived on campus to conduct the Bach B-minor Mass. He chose McNair as the soprano soloist. Shaw, known as a demanding taskmaster, was captivated by her voice and exuberant spirit and their relationship flourished. Under his direction, she made her European debut at the St. Moritz Festival in Switzerland and debuts at the New York Philharmonic, San Francisco Symphony, and many other venues from 1982 to 1989. Her first recording, made with Shaw in 1982, was nominated for a Grammy Award—a prestigious honor presented annually by the National Academy of Recording Arts and Sciences. He remained a mentor and friend until his death in 1999. "He literally picked me up out of the masses and gave me many, many chances," McNair says. "If it hadn't been for Robert Shaw, I would be a singing waitress pouring coffee in upstate New York somewhere." In 1991, McNair sang on the program when Shaw was given a Kennedy Center honor.

Early on, McNair decided not to enter major competitions until she knew she could win. She waited until 1982 to enter the Metropolitan Opera auditions and the San Francisco Opera auditions, highly competitive competitions. She won them both. It did not occur to her at the time that winning the Met auditions was unlikely after taking singing lessons for only five years. But the improbable happened. Also in 1982, McNair debuted at the Mostly Mozart Festival at Lincoln Center in New York City, performing in a Haydn opera. Professional manager Ann Colbert visited her in the dressing room after the show. She said, "Young lady, do you have a manager? If not, come and see me." Six weeks later, McNair hired her. Colbert, who was about 80 at the time, was an Old World–style manager with high-level clientele that included thirty-three-time Grammy winner Sir Georg Solti, legendary soprano Dame Joan Sutherland, and cellist Janos Starker. Although her roster boasted some of the biggest stars in the business, Colbert gave McNair an incredible amount of attention.

As her talent bloomed, McNair's confidence kept pace. With the flush of success from a number of professional performances, she gained poise befitting the stature of a talented, beautiful young woman. She graduated from IU with distinction in 1983, with a master's degree in music and a concentration in vocal performance.

In 1986, McNair married Hal France, a pianist and conductor. The couple, who did not have children, lived in the New York area but traveled extensively. McNair performed throughout the world, while France assumed leadership roles at various venues including the Orlando Philharmonic Orchestra and an opera company in Omaha, Nebraska. After eighteen years, France abruptly walked out of the marriage. McNair was devastated. "I was dragged to divorce court . . . kicking and screaming. That night, I cried so hard I hit the silent scream," says McNair.

For years, McNair was lauded throughout the world for her mastery of classical music as she sang operas and performed with symphonies. In 1990, she was named the first recipient of the Marian Anderson Award, named for a legendary contralto best remembered for her stirring performance on the steps of the Lincoln Memorial in 1939. The award, presented by the John F. Kennedy Center for Performing Arts and the Fairfield County Community Foundation in Connecticut, honors American singers of great promise who have achieved success in opera, in recital, and in the orchestral repertory.

But the classical music genre no longer seemed to fit. Songs from "The Great American Songbook" were always a part of her repertoire, but the increased exposure for this music during 1998, Gershwin's centennial year, really tugged at her heart. In 1999, McNair was rehearsing for her role of Cleopatra in Handel's *Julius Caesar* at the Metropolitan

Opera, working on "V'adoro pupille," a seductive aria in the second act, when she realized that instead of trying to seduce Caesar, she really wanted to perform a song like the Gershwin standard "Embraceable You." By then in her early 40s, she had spent her career duly following the advice of her publicist, her managers, and the record company without regard to the desires of her soul. So she made a second pleasure-driven decision.

Within the space of a few years, McNair reinvented herself "to be the me I wanted to be." Out of this innovation came her one-woman show, popular at supper clubs and cabarets including Feinstein's at the Regency, the Oak Room at the Algonquin, and the Carlyle in New York. The opera phase is completely closed. "After twenty years in opera—twenty more years than I ever dreamed I'd have—I chose to discontinue my opera career. I put it in a beautiful box, wrapped it up with a gorgeous bow, and said thank you very much. I put the box on a shelf to be remembered with great affection and fondness." She plans to spend the next twenty years "being me." She pays homage to her opera past by performing snippets of Handel or Mozart while discussing her transition into musical theater. And, of course, she plays her violin. The sixty-minute show is accompanied by a pianist and a bass player.

Rex Reed of the *New York Observer* reviewed one of her performances: "What a glowing surprise to find Ms. McNair not only in such splendid voice, but thrillingly adept at exploring the subtexts of songs in a dozen variable moods. For a classical singer making a segue into the art of the popular song, her phrasing is exemplary. Her modulations are inspired. . . . She knows how to rev up the power when it's needed and then soft-pedal the tremolo for subtlety. She has a sense of humor. She is an accomplished violinist who can make a miniature fiddle sound like bluegrass. . . . I could get used to this kind of ecstasy."

During her career, McNair has made more than seventy recordings, including many complete operas, although she hasn't recorded a classical music track since 1998. During her classical music heyday, she was nominated for nine Grammys and won twice. In 1993, she won Best

Opera Recording for the Handel opera *Semele*, and in 1995 she was named Best Classical Vocal Soloist for a recording of songs by Henry Purcell. Her newer CDs reflect the career change. She is especially proud of her two CDs with Sir André Previn, "Sure Thing, the Jerome Kern Songbook," which was released in 1994, and "Come Rain or Come Shine: The Harold Arlen Songbook," released in 1996. Previn, who for seven decades has been a renowned conductor and pianist, thrives in many musical neighborhoods, including pop and jazz. Those songbooks are among her favorite recordings. McNair also has recorded two Christmas CD projects released in 2008, one with Chicago pianist Kevin Cole and another in collaboration with the Wheaton Concert Choir, recorded in a church with near-perfect acoustics, as a tribute to her alma mater.

★ ★ ★

McNair was still reeling from her divorce that day in May 2006 when she was diagnosed with breast cancer. Just six months after a clear mammogram, the aggressive cancer had reached Stage III, an often irreversible condition where the cancer has spread to the lymph nodes. Stage IV is referred to as advanced stage. There is no Stage V. Living in New York at the time, she sought treatment at Sloan Kettering, a premier cancer hospital. But Sloan Kettering did not accept her health insurance, an individual plan provided to self-employed persons and independent contractors. So she chose to move home to Ohio for her cancer treatments at Ohio State University's James Cancer Center.

She underwent two months of intravenous chemotherapy with Adriamycin and cyclophosphamide, a chemical cocktail commonly known as AC. "AC is the worst, ugliest, and most hateful chemotherapy," McNair says. She had a mastectomy, followed by additional chemotherapy, then four additional cancer operations within the space of seven months. In July 2006, she was given six months to live. Later that year she was told again that she had very little time left. Two years later, she is still in chemo—this time Herceptin, which is not as debilitating as AC.

While going through chemotherapy in 2006, McNair cancelled all of her concerts and professional appearances and put her career on the shelf. She couldn't work. Many days she couldn't get out of bed. While she was coping with these tragic new realities, she got a job offer from Gwyn Richards, the dean of Indiana University's School of Music. He offered her a place on the faculty. "If you're too sick to work, that's okay, just come be here and let us help," Richards said. McNair had a fondness for her alma mater and had been assisting the dean in fundraising activities since 2001. So in August 2006, while undergoing treatment, McNair joined the faculty of the recently dubbed Jacobs School of Music at Indiana University and moved her permanent residence to Bloomington, Indiana. Now she is a teacher and mentor there, teaching an undergraduate opera workshop and an undergraduate English diction course for singers. She also tutors a number of private students. McNair is proud of the impact she has on already-good students. "I have twenty-five years of stuff packed in my head," she says. "Sharing it is an indescribable joy."

Despite her disease and the sometimes-difficult treatment, McNair fully expects to enjoy a long life. If attitude has a bearing, it is no wonder that she has beaten the odds. She defines her days simply. "Any day they are not sticking a needle in me is a great day," McNair said. "Cancer is one of the best things that's ever happened to me. It is a perspective-giver like nothing else I have experienced. Cancer has taught me about who I am and what I want. It has taught me that I can find paradise in the midst of trauma; I just have to be willing to try. Besides that, I would never have become a short-haired, spiky blond if it hadn't been for cancer." Before losing her hair to chemo, she cut fourteen inches of her brown hair and donated it to Locks of Love, a not-for-profit organization that provides hairpieces to financially disadvantaged children suffering from long-term medical hair loss.

She continues to defy her cancer by throwing parties. As she vowed when diagnosed, McNair gave a dinner party the night before her first chemotherapy session and a month later threw a head-shaving party.

Her friends feted her four days after her mastectomy. Eventually, "I'm going to have an 'I kicked cancer in the butt' party," she promises. "That's how I've chosen to deal with it. I chose to have fun with the very few things about cancer that you can have fun with." She credits her "guardian angel" girlfriends from around the country who have surrounded her with support, calling that encouragement the greatest gift she's ever had.

That's saying something, considering how blessed McNair has been. In July 1997, McNair met First Lady Hillary Clinton at the Salzburg Festival, where McNair was performing. She was invited to sing at a reception held by the Austrians for President Bill Clinton and his wife, who in turn invited her to reprise her performance at the White House. Unfortunately, the Monica Lewinsky scandal broke before her appearance could be scheduled. Then in May 1999, at the invitation of Justice Sandra Day O'Connor, McNair entertained the United States Supreme Court family and friends in the Supreme Court Building. That same year, McNair received the Governor's Award presented by Ohio governor Bob Taft. Fellow Ohio native John Glenn, the first astronaut to orbit the earth, also was given a Governor's Award the same evening.

The next year, McNair was chosen by Riccardo Muti, a famous Italian conductor, to perform with the Vienna Philharmonic at Pope John Paul II's 80th birthday party given by the Austrian Embassy. It was a remarkable experience for McNair, who is deeply spiritual. "I practice religion outside of its many boxes, but being in the arts you learn at a very early age that there is something larger than us going on," she says. She taps into that source with her music.

Throughout her busy career and even while dealing with the challenge of cancer, McNair has always remembered her community. In Bloomington, she supports the Shalom Center, which aids the poor and homeless. She is also a large donor to the Monroe County Humane Association. In honor of her father, she named two rooms of the Salvation Army's Dewald Community Center in her hometown of Mansfield. She also is a supporter of Over the Rainbow, a Chicago organization that builds apartments for severely disabled adults, and she provides financial assistance for a few graduate students at IU. "Singing is what gives my life happiness, pleasure, and joy," McNair says. "Giving is what gives my life meaning."

In 2007, McNair was presented with the Gaudium Award by the Breukelein Institute of New York, a not-for-profit entity whose chief concern is the poor, particularly children. The Gaudium Award has been given to men and women whose lives have "illuminated the horizon of human experience" through their extraordinary vocation in the arts and public service. McNair's tax attorney gently reminds her that she sings more performances for free than for pay.

Given her lifelong interest in sports, it isn't surprising that McNair can be seen singing "The Star Spangled Banner" at IU basketball games. Of course, she stays to watch the games, too. She also sings the national anthem at IU's Little 500 bicycle race, a popular event that gained fame in the 1979 movie *Breaking Away*.

McNair credits her piano teacher, Elizabeth Pastor, who inspired her and inspires her to this day. At 9, she decided she wanted to be just like Miss Pastor. She also cites Howard Beebe, her violin teacher, John Wustman, her art song coach, Virginia Zeani, her opera teacher, and Eileen Farrell, her jazz and pop coach, as positive influences.

Even as she has placed cancer in proper perspective, she is dealing with the inner demons and self-criticism of growing old in the music business. "I'm not young, I'm not news. I've been around for twenty-five years," she says. Indeed, McNair has made her living as a singer for a quarter of a century, much of that on the highest level. "Self-doubts are healthy. It makes you better and it makes you work harder," she added. "Self-doubts, self-analysis, self-knowledge, always make you stronger."

Perhaps McNair will quiet those demons as she continues to perform "in her own skin," on her own terms. "As close to death as I have been, I get to define how I do the rest of this. That's the great part. I'm calling the shots now. Cancer redefines how one lives," says McNair. In her new genre, there is no age limit—as proven by veteran performers Lena Horne, Ella Fitzgerald, and Barbara Cook, who was still performing at 81.

McNair spent July 2007 at the Ravinia Festival in Chicago, performing in *The Most Happy Fella*. Rehearsing and singing the Frank Loesser opera-cum-musical with George Hearn, a Broadway legend, were happy days for McNair. Her performance prompted the festival's CEO, Welz Kauffman, to comment that McNair "brought all of her trademark vocal beauty plus the physical presence that proved both glamorous and frisky, beguiling her men in the ear and the eye."

One of the cherished honors that McNair has been given is an honorary doctorate bestowed by Indiana University's School of Music in 1998. She delivered the commencement address to new graduates, defining her faith by saying, "Take the leap and the net will appear." Violin virtuoso, classical singer, cabaret performer, cancer survivor—whatever the high wire, Sylvia McNair has taken the leap many times. And this transplanted Hoosier has not missed the net yet.

Sharon Rivenbark

Sock It to Me

People are drawn to Indiana for many reasons, employment and economic opportunity chief among them. But for Sharon Rivenbark, the decision to move to the Hoosier state was all about family. Working as a school teacher in Belleville, Illinois, Rivenbark often would dream of living in an idyllic setting where her family could cultivate a garden and keep cows and chickens to provide for their own basic needs. She longed to raise her children in a place where they could enjoy the unfettered freedom of riding horses and motorcycles, and where they could experience the simple, wholesome "country living" romanticized in John Denver songs of the day. She found the place on a visit to rustic Nashville, Indiana.

So in 1974, Rivenbark and her husband at the time packed up their family and moved to the charming Brown County town. She has never looked back. Nearly thirty-five years later, Rivenbark has spun that family-first philosophy into a successful business enterprise—For Bare Feet, the nation's leading producer of licensed socks and promotional footwear. Still living and working in Brown County, her love for the area's captivating country charm remains undiminished. But Rivenbark's odyssey from rural fifth-grade teacher to corporate CEO was anything but simple. It is a heroic tale filled with struggle and triumph—and tinged with tragedy.

★ ★ ★

Born October 6, 1937, Rivenbark started out as a Trainer—personally, as Trainer is her family name, and professionally, because as professional educators, training is exactly what her people have done for several generations. Her father, Curtis, was superintendent of the local school district, and nine of her aunts and uncles were teachers, principals, or coaches. Rivenbark married and began her family before earning a bachelor's degree in elementary education from Southern Illinois University in 1969, then began her career as a first-grade teacher. She got her master's degree the following year.

Her younger brother Curt, meanwhile, had given up teaching to try his hand at sales. His territory included Indiana and western Ohio. When the strain of traveling from his home in western Illinois began taking its toll, he decided to move to a central location. He chose Nashville, Indiana. Unlike its well-known namesake in Tennessee, Indiana's Nashville has no connection with the country music industry, but it is a decidedly "country" community. Long known as an artistic enclave, Nashville is nestled amid Brown County's lush, rolling hills. Its rural charm captivated Trainer every time he passed through while making his sales rounds. He glowingly described the locale to his sister back in Belleville, urging her to visit and see for herself. And one summer's day in 1973, Rivenbark and several family members did just that. By nightfall, she was as smitten by the town's charms as her brother had been. The next year, she moved her family to Nashville.

Rivenbark quickly found work as a fifth-grade language arts teacher in the Brown County public school system, working with children whose education, for a variety of reasons, was academically deficient. She strove to identify these problem areas and deliver the appropriate remediation. The work was rewarding and prepared her somewhat for the challenges that lay ahead.

By the early 1980s, Rivenbark was living the country life she had always wanted. She was a respected educator and had become a single mother of five. "I don't do well with male dogs or husbands," she explains with a mischievous smile.

When her 16-year-old son, Tim Magnuson, began complaining of severe headaches, Rivenbark wondered if it had anything to do with a lesion that had appeared on his face when he was a toddler. Indeed, the growth a dermatologist had refused to remove turned out to be an early indicator of what eventually was diagnosed in the teenager as tuberous sclerosis complex, or TSC. Also called Bourneville's disease, it is a rare, genetic condition that causes noncancerous tumors to grow in the brain and other vital organs. Symptoms often include seizures and severe learning and behavioral problems. More than half of those with the condition also have developmental disorders.

After the diagnosis, Tim was admitted to Indiana University Hospital for surgery to place a small drainage tube in an area of his brain that had been choked off by one of the growths. Because the doctors agreed to release Tim after the surgery so he could attend a showing of his prize calf at a 4-H competition, Rivenbark assumed that the operation had been a success. She was wrong. Tim's doctors had released him because there was little they could do medically. They could not remove the growths without damaging vital portions of his brain.

Years of experimentation and testing followed, some carried out by Rivenbark herself. As part of her master's degree coursework, she had learned how to administer various intelligence assessment tests. To practice, Rivenbark would test her own children, along with any nieces or nephews she could persuade to help her. That's how she knew that before his condition worsened, Tim's IQ had been quite high—nearly 150. He completed high school without trouble, but by the time he enrolled at Indiana University's nearby Bloomington campus in September 1983, his score had dropped to 110. Rivenbark's hopes that he would someday earn a medical degree were dashed.

That October, Rivenbark received a panicked call from Tim's roommates. They couldn't awaken him. Rivenbark enlisted an emergency vehicle from the local hospital and rushed to pick up Tim in Bloomington.

He was quickly transported to Indianapolis, some sixty miles away, where he underwent another operation. This time the news was grim.

"Tim's condition has worsened," she was told. "Eventually he could become severely mentally retarded. You're going to need some assistance with this." Rivenbark was provided with the name of a state agency that would help her son find some type of occupational therapy. He would not be mentally able to continue with his studies. She was devastated by the news, but when she heard a hospital worker actually mention the word "basket-weaving" while discussing occupational options for him, something inside of her clicked.

"No way," she told herself. There was no possible way that she was going to watch Tim fade away before her eyes. She would never allow her son to be placed into an institution. Instead, she would put him into business. Rivenbark understood that the most important thing she could give her ailing son was a sense of self-esteem and personal respect. Since college was out of the question, Tim would not be able to achieve those benefits by becoming a lawyer or a doctor. He didn't need a degree to become a businessman, however. But what sort of business? That was the question.

Nashville's main street is lined with quaint boutiques and craft shops, almost all locally owned. And in autumn, when thousands of tourists descend upon Brown County during their annual pilgrimage to witness the blazing fall colors, the streets and stores fill to capacity. Rivenbark thought a Nashville tourist shop would be just the ticket for Tim. Such a business could quickly become self-sustaining and would not require a great deal of start-up capital. If it just made enough money to break even, that would be great, she thought. "I was looking for a place that would list Tim's name as the proprietor on the sign above the door," she explained. "I wanted him to experience a sense of pride."

Rivenbark considered and rejected several possibilities—including a T-shirt shop and a restaurant—before hitting upon an idea she thought might just be crazy enough to work. The most successful boutiques were the ones where merchandise was made on-site; customers could watch a quilt being pieced together or a doily being crocheted, for example, and purchase it when it was finished. In searching for something she and her son could make and sell, Rivenbark remembered a family trip to Gatlinburg, Tennessee, where she had been captivated at the sight of an antique knitting machine chugging along in a store window. The store was taking a cue from other tourist shops that placed a fudge-making machine in their front windows to attract customers. But instead of fudge, this machine made socks.

The idea seemed perfect for Tim. He could certainly operate the knitting machine, and he could train someone else to operate it for him if and when that became necessary. So Rivenbark began her hunt for an antique sock-knitting machine. She phoned more than a dozen stocking and sock makers around the country before being referred to a used machinery dealer. Finding a sympathetic ear, Rivenbark related Tim's story and soon became the proud owner of a broken-down relic known as a Banner Full Cushion Circular Sock Machine. Built during the 1870s by a long-defunct Pawtucket, Rhode Island, manufacturer, the machine was in need of extensive restoration before it could be used. An equipment dealer in High Point, North Carolina, provided Rivenbark with the arcane spare parts she needed and helped her locate the particular yarn required by the machine. He went even further by dispatching an associate to Indiana to conduct the needed repairs and to train Tim to operate the machine.

Before long, Rivenbark had a storefront in Nashville's Antique Alley and an operational vintage sock-knitting machine calculated to intrigue passersby. There was one more missing piece: cash. She didn't have enough to purchase the machine and yarn and pay the first month's rent. Fortunately, Rivenbark got a $1,200 loan from her parents to use as start-up capital for the fledgling venture.

With his mother's help, Tim opened the sock store in time for the 1984 spring tourist season. They selected the name "For Bare Feet." As anticipated, visitors walking by the tiny shop were intrigued, first by the antique knitting machine rhythmically puttering away and then by the novel idea of socks as a gift item. In addition to the solid-color socks that were produced in the store, For Bare Feet sold personalized and novelty socks made elsewhere. The colorful new designs stimulated sales and, in a matter of months, the store was operating in the black. In fact, business was so strong that first year, For Bare Feet remained open during the winter months—the off-season for most Nashville tourist shops.

Word of Tim and his success with the Nashville sock store spread. During the summer of 1984, the director of the Indiana University student bookstore in Bloomington helped Rivenbark obtain the license necessary to imprint IU logos, slogans, and other copyrighted material onto her socks. The "Go Big Red" socks were a hit as students wore them proudly to football games and around campus. The idea of using socks as a means of self-expression—a well-heeled alternative to baseball caps, bumper stickers, and T-shirts, if you will—soon caught on. Before long, For Bare Feet was producing custom socks for many of the school's sororities and fraternities.

The store got another break that fall, when Rivenbark received a phone call from Indianapolis: "My wife and I visited your shop last weekend when we were in Nashville," the caller explained. "We really liked all the unique socks and I was wondering if you ever sold them anywhere other than from your shop." Rivenbark told him about the socks available at the IU Bookstore and discovered the purpose of his call. The man, a merchandising director for Simon Property Group in Indianapolis, wanted to know if For Bare Feet would be interested in setting up a kiosk at the Bloomington Mall to sell seasonal socks during the Christmas shopping season. At the time, Simon was on its way to becoming the world's largest developer of regional shopping centers. Today, it operates 380 properties in 39 states and 52 countries. Talk about getting your foot in the door.

Rivenbark quickly grabbed the opportunity and the kiosk proved so successful that she and Tim went on to set up shop in several more nearby Simon malls.

While Tim's condition had not improved, he was exhibiting very few symptoms during this period. His enthusiasm for the business was clearly serving to stave off the debilitating effects of his illness.

Before that incredible first year was over, Rivenbark had initiated wholesale operations, supplying custom socks to a number of specialty boutiques around the state. Buyers from such stores regularly gravitated to Nashville in search of unusual items to stock their shelves. For Bare Feet's socks, with their unique styles and patterns, were an instant hit with this crowd, and Rivenbark and Tim quickly discovered that it was much more lucrative to sell socks by the dozen than by the pair. The business had exploded exponentially from a quaint tourist gift shop to a regional wholesale distributorship—all in less than a year.

Another major milestone was Rivenbark's first trip to an industry trade show in Chicago in 1985. She had decided that given the "country" appeal of her product line, she'd be better off at the gift show than the apparel show being held at the same time. So, using wooden crates as display shelving, Rivenbark showed off her unique line of socks to buyers from around the world. Other vendors stopped by her booth and offered advice as she was setting up for the show: "These are really cute, but you should be at the apparel show," they told her. She didn't listen. Since no one had ever considered making a gift item out of socks before, she was carving out a whole new product category. The strategy paid off. For Bare Feet's booth attracted a great amount of interest and she left the show with new customers' orders in hand.

In order to allow enough time to establish the new business for Tim, Rivenbark had requested and been granted a one-year leave of absence from her teaching position. At the conclusion of that whirlwind year, Rivenbark found herself sitting amid the dozens of sock boxes that now filled her home, evidence of a booming new business that was growing increasingly out of control. When the time came for her to resume her teaching career, Rivenbark realized that she had reached a critical crossroads.

"Things were just too hectic and disorganized for me to turn the business over to Tim at that time," she explains. "I felt that if I could just have another year away from teaching, I could get things on an even keel and then Tim could run it." She met with school administrators to request a second year's leave of absence. They turned her down and Rivenbark submitted her resignation.

During that first year, Rivenbark had not counted her own time as an ongoing business expense since she regarded it as a start-up cost. But now things had changed. With Tim and two of his siblings still living at home, the business would need to generate enough to keep paying her a salary. Could the business survive this new expense? Rivenbark had no idea. Unlike most entrepreneurs, Rivenbark had neither a business degree nor a background in business. Her experience in education did not equip her for the rigors of owning a small business—not in the traditional sense, at least. She knew nothing about payroll taxes or liability insurance or inventory control. She learned whatever she could on the job.

Fortunately, with the support of friends including Nashville attorney Andy Szakaly, Rivenbark was able to avoid many of the pitfalls that typically plague other start-ups—such as how to deal with giant corporate competitors. Rivenbark called Szakaly one day after receiving a threatening letter from attorneys representing retail powerhouse Lazarus Department Stores and one of its sock vendors. A For Bare Feet kiosk had been positioned directly in front of the entrance to a Lazarus store at a Simon mall. Sales at the kiosk were so brisk that they began eating into Lazarus's sock business. The attorneys' letter instructed Rivenbark to cease all operations or face legal action on the grounds of copyright infringement. Lazarus claimed that the pair of footprints that For Bare Feet was using to identify its product line too closely resembled the vendor's registered trademark.

"What do we do, Andy?" Rivenbark asked the attorney.

"You can fight it in court and you'll probably win since your logo looks nothing like theirs," he advised. "Their complaint is bogus."

"That's good news," she enthusiastically replied.

"No, it's not." Szakaly went on. "They'll be able to get an injunction to close you down while the case is pending and that could mean months. You'll be out of business during Christmas—which is exactly what they want. On top of that, you would need a major cash supply in order to fight them."

"So what do we do?" she demanded.

"Change your logo," he said. And so she did. Originally a pair of bare feet, the logo was redesigned in the shape of a single footprint. For Bare Feet still uses it today.

Despite such challenges, the business continued to grow and by 1986 Tim had opened stores in five shopping malls. He had a steady girl-friend, his health remained stable, and he continued to mystify doctors with his lack of symptoms. Then the headaches began again. That October, Tim underwent an operation to clear the drainage tube still imbedded in his head. Another operation followed on Christmas Eve. Despite their earlier reluctance, the doctors felt that they had no choice and attempted to excise the growths in Tim's brain. The ordeal left the young man in a coma, dependent upon life support equipment to keep him alive. On January 12, 1987, Rivenbark and her other children vis-ited Tim for the last time as they bid him a tearful good-bye.

"Tim was gone," Rivenbark recalls, "and there was no question at that moment that the business would continue. It was all I had left of him."

Rivenbark's family grew even closer after Tim's death. Her daughter Kelly, in college at the time, continued to help out at the business just as she had done during high school. Rivenbark saw the business contin-ue to thrive. As demand grew, she purchased six Amy Brand knitting machines at a sock mill in North Carolina capable of running nonstop, twenty-four hours a day, seven days a week, and contracted with the mill to operate the machines.

Rivenbark's daughter Sheree's husband, Karl Mills, joined the busi-ness in 1985 after completing a computer-technology degree at Indiana University. Within weeks of graduation, he left for North Carolina to work as an apprentice in the For Bare Feet operation. Mills spent week-days in North Carolina learning how to operate the machines and returned to his family in Indiana on weekends. Rivenbark noticed that production would drop off dramatically whenever he was gone. One Saturday in late 1987, Rivenbark and Mills decided to conduct a surprise visit to the East Coast sock-making operation. They were in for a shock. The owner of the mill was using the For Bare Feet machines on the weekends to make socks and sell them to local high schools. Rivenbark and her son-in-law wasted no time. They headed straight for the local U-Haul outlet, then drove back to the factory and loaded up their equipment. When they got back to Brown County, Rivenbark and Mills delivered the machines to the former Helmsburg High School, an old building that was serving as For Bare Feet's warehouse and corporate office. After moving the machines into the gymnasium of the old school, they were cranking out socks after only a twenty-four-hour interruption in production.

Mills' technological skills proved to be an asset when the company moved up to Italian Sangiacomo computerized knitting machines in the 1990s. He was able to alter the mechanics and reprogram the devices so they produced totally unique designs and patterns.

In 1992, Rivenbark's daughter Kelly Baugh, fresh from IU, joined the company full time as vice president of sales. Rivenbark and Baugh were aware that the company would regularly experience a major slowdown in production during the winter months, often resulting in employee layoffs. Both felt that had to change. Recognizing that the sport-licensing market enjoyed a year-round selling season, mother and daughter decided to aggressively pursue it. Baugh pitched For Bare Feet's superior product line to all of the nation's sports licensing powers, eventually winning team licenses from the NBA in 1996. Now the company has similar deals with the NFL, NHL, Major League Baseball, and NASCAR, along with an ever-expanding collection of colleges and universities. When For Bare Feet began producing lucrative logo-emblazoned socks, the wide world of opportunity got a little wider.

Such contracts have opened the door to distribution agreements with major national retailers such as Footlocker and The Finish Line. For Bare Feet also benefits from online sales via websites such as espn.go.com and nhlshop.com. Today, the company is divided into two main product divisions: team/university socks and novelty socks. Custom orders are produced for such diverse customers as dog breeding organizations and AIDS awareness groups.

Today, three of Rivenbark's daughters work at the company, where she remains CEO: Baugh is still overseeing sales, Tina Bode is vice president of operations, and Mandy Zellmer serves as president. Her fourth daughter, Sheree Mills, is a teacher. All four of her sons-in-law work for the company. The oldest of Rivenbark's eleven grandchildren help out during the summer months. In the past twenty-four years, For Bare Feet has grown to become a true family-owned enterprise, something Rivenbark attributes to the force of Tim's legacy. She also credits it as a positive force in the community, as the company provides 140 jobs and economic opportunity to rural Brown County, Indiana.

The shop in Antique Alley is still open, although socks are no longer made on site. The old Banner Knitting Machine that first attracted customers is on display in the Helmsburg factory. It is pointed out with pride during the regular tours the company provides to the public. A photo of Tim working on the machine is mounted next to it.

It has been more than two decades since a determined Brown County schoolteacher bravely opened a tiny tourist boutique to provide her ailing son with something very precious, the pride of ownership. While many would marvel at such a gift, Sharon Rivenbark sees it as more of an opportunity than a sacrifice. "Whatever I gave to Tim," she explains, "has been given back to me by him a million times over. Since his loss—and sometimes I get the feeling he's still very much with us—Tim has served as the inspiration and guiding light for everyone associated with this company. His life was filled with so much promise and potential that today I feel that our success represents a fulfillment of his dreams. And what greater gift is there than that?"

Alecia A. DeCoudreaux

Living Her Dreams

As a child in the late 1950s and early 1960s, Alecia DeCoudreaux assumed her mother was being frugal and efficient, loading the car with food and a portable toilet when her family drove from Chicago to the Mississippi coast to visit her father's relatives. Later, she realized it was a necessity, since blacks were not welcome in most dining establishments along many of the roads that led south. Despite growing up amid the turmoil of the civil rights movement—or perhaps because of it—DeCoudreaux dreamed big from an early age. At 6, she decided she would become a lawyer. Further inspired by her third-grade teacher, Ms. Thomas, who taught school because she could not support herself as a black female attorney, DeCoudreaux relentlessly pursued her dream—all the way to a senior leadership position at pharmaceutical powerhouse Eli Lilly and Company.

★ ★ ★

Born on the rough-and-tumble south side of Chicago in 1954, DeCoudreaux, along with her older brother, John, was raised in a "multi-parent" household after their parents separated. Her mother, Viola, was the youngest of eight children, so DeCoudreaux received plenty of parenting from her close-knit family of uncles, aunts, and grandparents. She lived in an all-black neighborhood and attended

Catholic school in Chicago most of the year. During summer months, she resided in what she describes as an idyllic setting on Cape Cod, Massachusetts, where her mother's family had settled after emigrating from Africa's Cape Verde Islands more than a hundred years ago.

"Growing up, I had the best of both worlds," DeCoudreaux recalls. "My mother would take me to art and science museums in Chicago during the school year. Then as soon as school was out my uncle would drive from Massachusetts and take me back to live with my grandmother and other family members on Cape Cod."

Still, her formative years were not entirely serene. Her parents split up when she was 6, and she had little contact with her father after that. She last saw him in 1971, twenty years before his death. As a child, DeCoudreaux also experienced racial discrimination, although she was not fully conscious of what was happening at the time. The home-packed meals during trips to visit her father's family in Pass Christian, Mississippi, were one example. She also keenly remembers the assassination of Martin Luther King Jr. and the 1968 race riots in Chicago. Then there were the school outings to rural Illinois and Wisconsin, where the students from her all-black elementary school were introduced to white families.

"The white children wanted to touch us, like we were the objects of 'Show and Tell.' I didn't like that at all," DeCoudreaux recalls. "It was only much later that I understood what the nuns were trying to do: to educate the white children, to broaden their experience and understanding, just as ours was being broadened.

"These are all events that affect you and about which you have a greater understanding as you mature."

Even so, she probably was better equipped to deal with the racially charged 1960s than most her age because she had been raised in both white and black cultures. Although both of her parents were black, DeCoudreaux's extended family included a number of mixed-race couples; interracial relationships were not as uncommon in New England as they were in the Midwest and South in the 1960s.

DeCoudreaux attended high school at Chicago's Academy of Our Lady, also known as Longwood Academy. The integrated all-girls Catholic school was operated by the School Sisters of Notre Dame, an order of nuns. She is grateful for her twelve years of Catholic education, which she says taught her discipline of "mind and body"—something that continues to help her focus on her work and commitments. She quickly learned the importance of schedules and punctuality. She realized there were consequences if deadlines were missed. DeCoudreaux believes all that training enabled her to make the most of her time and talent.

"I loved to watch Perry Mason on television," she says. "I think my family always thought that I would be a lawyer. They saw me as argumentative, while I thought I was merely being persuasive."

She admits to having a competitive nature, something that developed as she tried to keep up with her brother and more than a dozen older cousins. "I was always the smallest and youngest of the group," DeCoudreaux says.

Her childhood passions included cooking, reading, and picking strawberries during her summer months in Massachusetts. "In Chicago, my grandmother would take me to the public library on Friday afternoons and allow me to check out as many books as I wanted so I could read them throughout the week. On the way, we would stop at a newsstand and I'd purchase two comic books to read right away."

At Longwood Academy, DeCoudreaux was a member of the school's National Honor Society and Future Teachers Association. (There was no future lawyers club.) She enjoyed playing the piano for plays and musicals. Before graduating in 1972, she applied to a handful of elite women's colleges on the East Coast after becoming aware of their excellent reputations during her time in Massachusetts. However, she was surprised when she was accepted at Wellesley College in Wellesley, Massachusetts, because she thought her admission interview had not gone well.

"I was very critical of the Catholic Church," DeCoudreaux recalls.

"During my Wellesley admissions interview, I shared how outraged I was over its treatment of women and the poor. When the Church had so much wealth, I couldn't understand why it allowed golden chalices to be used when the poor needed help. The Church also excluded women from full participation in the sacraments.

"The admissions interviewer told me later that my interview had helped me gain admission. I guess she was impressed by how well I had been able to articulate my views, although I look back upon them now and realize that perhaps some of my outrage at the Church was based upon naïveté."

DeCoudreaux was in the minority again at Wellesley, as one of forty-six black students in a class of about five hundred. She paid for school through a mixture of scholarships, loans, and work. In her free time, she was involved with Ethos, the black student organization on campus. She graduated in 1976 with a bachelor's degree in English and political science. From Wellesley, DeCoudreaux immediately enrolled at Indiana University's School of Law in Bloomington, where she studied for the next twenty-seven months, taking no breaks from the time she began in May 1976. She received her law degree in August 1978.

DeCoudreaux's first job out of law school was with San Francisco–based Pillsbury, Madison and Sutro, one of the largest and most prestigious law firms on the West Coast. She chose San Francisco after traveling there in 1978 to visit the man she ultimately married and later divorced. DeCoudreaux fell in love with the Bay Area and applied for a position with PM&S. She practiced with the firm for two years, handling mostly antitrust cases.

In 1980 her husband, who worked for Eli Lilly and Co., was transferred to Indianapolis and she returned to Indiana with him. Soon after, he took her résumé to his employer. The pharmaceutical giant saw DeCoudreaux's potential and hired her. She looked forward to making the leap from private practice to corporate law, thinking she would try that for a couple of years before moving on. She never imagined she would still be there nearly three decades later.

"During the first several months with Eli Lilly, I did not have a specific assignment. I did odd bits of work that no one else really wanted to do," DeCoudreaux says. "The company was reorganizing the law division and its managers knew there soon would be a position for me. It was not the best beginning, but I have no regrets given the work I've been able to do ever since."

One of only a handful of publicly traded Fortune 500 companies in Indiana, Lilly employs about forty thousand people worldwide to make and distribute drugs, including the antidepressant Prozac. Regularly included in *Fortune* magazine's list of the top hundred companies to work for in the United States, Lilly was recognized by *Barron's* magazine in 2006 as one of the five hundred best-managed companies in the country.

Since joining Lilly in 1980, DeCoudreaux has taken on a number of different responsibilities: She handled patent work as secretary and general counsel for Lilly subsidiary Advanced Cardiovascular Systems, Inc. in Santa Clara, California, then was promoted to director of community relations for Eli Lilly and Co. in 1990 before becoming its director for corporate affairs in 1992 and director of government relations in 1993. That position required her to move to Washington, D.C.

"I was in Washington at the start of the [President Bill] Clinton administration and there was significant activity going on with changes to health care policy," she says. "It was an exciting time and I believe I began to learn for the first time how laws are really made."

DeCoudreaux returned to Indiana in 1994, when she became executive director of Lilly's Medical Research Administration and later its Research Planning and Scientific Administration. In these roles, she was involved with the discovery and early development of new compounds through clinical trials with human patients. This process is the core mechanism by which new drugs ultimately become approved by the Food and Drug Administration for sale to the public.

In 1999, DeCoudreaux was named Lilly's secretary and deputy general counsel, holding that position until 2005, when she assumed the title and responsibilities of vice president and general counsel for Lilly USA, Eli Lilly and Co.'s largest division. In that position, DeCoudreaux oversees a legal department of about thirty employees, including attorneys and support staff, that counsels other departments on regulatory compliance, privacy matters, antitrust concerns, clinical research, and contracts. Her varied experience at the company has prepared her for whatever arises. "There is no typical day at Lilly," she said. "Every day presents new challenges. We work long, hard hours, but we love what we do."

Given that commitment, it is not surprising DeCoudreaux has infused her professional life with some of the lessons learned through personal experience—like the need to understand others' perspectives and respect diversity. She recalls a situation in the early 1980s, when she was among a group of Lilly attorneys and scientists meeting with regulators at the Food and Drug Administration's cramped Washington, D.C., offices. DeCoudreaux and the others—all well-dressed white men—were telling the diverse group of underpaid FDA employees what Lilly wanted them to know when it hit her: "We needed to understand their perspectives and concerns about improving patient outcomes if we expected them to understand ours."

Reflecting upon the experience more than two decades later, DeCoudreaux remarks, "I've never raised children, but I always thought that if you want them to listen to you, you should listen to them. The same is true about conducting business with customers, suppliers, and regulators."

DeCoudreaux's desire to be respectful of others' opinions and yet firm about her own has served her well. As one of the top African American women at Lilly, she believes it is her mission to be a daily provocateur, to make the company and its employees even better. "I am a bit of a perfectionist. I want to lead by example," she said. "I constantly question; I prod and raise issues that some may think about, but not always express.

"The challenges we face in the pharmaceutical industry, particularly concerns about drug costs and perceptions of us being more concerned about profits than patients, are uppermost in my mind. I want my colleagues to understand what other people have to deal with who don't necessarily have the medical and prescription drug coverage that we have as Lilly employees."

Community service is one way to accomplish that and, again, DeCoudreaux leads by example. Her volunteer duties require nearly as much energy and attention as her day job. That's little surprise, given her family's civic legacy. Her maternal grandmother came to the United States in the early twentieth century from the Cape Verde Islands off of the coast of West Africa. Although she was never fluent in English (speaking mainly Portuguese), she helped bring dozens of babies into the world as a midwife on Cape Cod. She was passionate about taking care of others in her community, and she has helped raise many children.

DeCoudreaux has followed in her grandmother's footsteps, serving the community as a member of Indianapolis's Capital Improvement Board of Managers and of the United Way of Central Indiana Women's Initiative board, and chairing Indianapolis Downtown Inc.'s board of directors. Past service includes years of volunteerism on behalf of organizations such as Big Brothers of Indianapolis, the IU Foundation, and the Indianapolis Campaign for Healthy Babies—just a sampling of the more than twenty not-for-profit and educational organizations DeCoudreaux has been involved with since the early 1990s. Despite this impressive record, she does not view her commitment to volunteerism as totally selfless.

"Every time I take on a new civic challenge, I gain a different perspective. I get a feeling of giving back, which is very important to me."

In 2007, she assumed her most public leadership position—chair of the board of trustees at Wellesley College. She joined her alma mater's board in 2002. Founded in 1870, Wellesley is one of the nation's elite liberal arts colleges, with about 36,000 living alumnae. Graduates include a "Who's Who" of women leaders in government, business, the media, and entertainment, such as U.S. senator Hillary Rodham

Clinton, former U.S. secretary of state and U.N. ambassador Madeleine Albright, national news reporters Cokie Roberts and Diane Sawyer, former Chinese nationalist leader Madam Chiang Kai-shek, and writer, movie producer, and actress Nora Ephron.

Many of DeCoudreaux's best friends are Wellesley graduates. One of the most important qualities she appreciates about her alma mater is the generations of alumnae whom she has come to know, not only through her work on the college's board of trustees but from the years she served on its alumnae association board of directors (1995 to 1998) and its national development and outreach council (1998–2002) and through campus reunions she regularly attends.

DeCoudreaux's list of awards is nearly as long as her string of volunteer commitments. She won a Spirit of Philanthropy Award in 1992, the Madam CJ Walker Award for Outstanding Achievement in 1993, a Girls Inc. Touchstone Award in 1997, the Indiana State Bar Association's Women in the Law Achievement Award in 1998, Indiana Bar Foundation's Fellow Award in 1999, Indiana University's Distinguished Alumni Service Award in 2003, the Archdiocese of Indianapolis's Community Service Award in 2006, Indianapolis Mayor's Community Service Award in 2006, a Hoosier Heritage Lifetime Achievement Award in 2006, and the *Indiana Lawyer*'s Distinguished Barrister Award in 2007.

DeCoudreaux attributes her professional and personal successes to a variety of factors: hard work, persistence, honesty, a willingness to take on new challenges—even an element of luck. Her many role models include her grandmother, her mother, her aunts, former Wellesley president Diane Chapman Walsh, and several colleagues at Lilly.

As a boss, she works to bring staff and colleagues together socially in "neutral territories" to build an esprit de corps. They've met at restaurants, picnicked in parks, and raced go-carts together. In recent years, she's helped establish Lilly's diversity leadership council and has sponsored all four of the company's retreats for women in leadership positions.

If she weren't an attorney and executive, DeCoudreaux confesses that her fantasy job would be as a restaurant owner. She has all the details in mind. "The restaurant would be near a large body of water and be open only four nights a week. I would grow 80 percent of the food served to my appreciative customers."

In the few hours each week that she's not deep in meetings, she manages to pursue her hobbies. "I'm an avid walker and I still like to play the piano and read, especially mysteries," DeCoudreaux said. Within that genre, she prefers culinary who-dun-its, novels from authors such as Diane Mott Davidson and Virginia Rich (a former food editor for the *Chicago Sun-Times*) or mysteries set in locations she loves, such as Philip Craig's series based on life on Martha's Vineyard.

"Also, almost every month I visit my mother and my aunt Anita, who is 92, at their homes on Cape Cod. I love spending time with them and the visits are never long enough." DeCoudreaux's mother left Chicago in the mid-1970s to return to Cape Cod, where she lives in the home in which she was born.

DeCoudreaux already knows what she would like to pursue when she retires. "I would love to do something in the field of education. My position as chair of the Wellesley board may help fulfill my itch, but I have a strong yearning to help young people, especially those who come from poor backgrounds, to understand how access to education can change their lives. That is one reason that I have such a great appreciation for Wellesley. It has a 'needs blind' admission policy. Students are admitted regardless of their ability to pay."

She also dreams of a day when she can travel more freely. In the past she has journeyed to Brazil, South Africa, Israel, and other far-flung locales. She and her mother plan to visit the Cape Verde Islands to locate and explore her grandparents' birthplace.

"I love going to places that are so very different from the United States. I think I have learned a great deal from witnessing incredible poverty and horrendous living conditions for people in other parts of the world. My niece is a Peace Corps volunteer. Seeing other parts of the world through her eyes has been very enlightening and given me a greater appreciation for how much we can do to be helpful abroad, as well as in our own communities."

DeCoudreaux's advice to young women reflects values she has embraced her entire life: "It is so important to know and understand yourself and to carry yourself with dignity and self-respect. If you do this, then you can expect it of others."

Divorced, DeCoudreaux gives the impression that a future spouse is not on her to-do list, at least not any time soon. She enjoys the freedom of being single and admits she wouldn't have the time to commit to her many interests if she were married. She has concluded that life without a partner, whether by choice or not, is another important reason for women to take control of their lives.

"I remember several years ago a colleague of mine learned that he had a terminal illness. He was told to go home, get his affairs in order, and return to the hospital. At home, he had to spend quite a bit of time teaching his wife how to pay bills and handle certain financial arrangements. This reinforced my belief that women need to be self-sufficient, to educate themselves, so that whatever happens to them they can take care of themselves and their families."

DeCoudreaux is determined to be independent, but always with the understanding that her obligations extend beyond merely taking care of herself. She is a model of the successful executive who also is compassionate and able to give freely despite her many professional responsibilities. Indiana is blessed to have her leadership and it appears that it will benefit from her strong commitment to "building a better community" for many years to come.

Jane Blaffer Owen

The Buckwheat Bride

I t was during America's last summer of innocence, in August 1941, that 25-year-old oil heiress Jane Blaffer became a buckwheat bride. A balmy westward wind rippled the tops of the wheat fields surrounding the tiny St. Anne, Ontario, church as Jane and her new husband, Kenneth Dale Owen, emerged to accept the warm embraces of a small contingent of family members and other well-wishers. The couple had decided to conduct their nuptials in St. Anne, where the Blaffer family owned a vacation home to which they retreated every August in order to escape Houston's oppressive heat. It was an ideal spot to begin a new life chapter. The beaming bride, whose wedding gown matched the undulating buckwheat's paler shade of white, now sported a new name that also rippled with history—and within it, a stunning irony.

Jane was the daughter of a celebrated "captain of American industry," Robert E. Lee Blaffer. Some thirty years earlier, Blaffer and business partner William Farish had merged their small Houston oil drilling concern with several others to found the Humble Oil Company. Humble Oil eventually evolved into Exxon, America's largest corporation and arguably the world's most monumental manifestation of capitalism.

Jane's new husband, on the other hand, was the great-great-grandson of a man who embodied the antithesis of capitalism, Robert Owen. Owen was an Englishman regarded by historians as the founder of

"utopian socialism," a nineteenth-century movement that counted among its adherents no less of a figure than Karl Marx. In fact, it was her new husband's family link to an early American socialist experiment that soon had the oil baron's daughter traveling from the wheat fields of Ontario to the cornfields of southwestern Indiana.

Today, Jane Blaffer Owen is known as Mrs. Jane by nearly everyone in New Harmony, Indiana, the town Robert Owen purchased in 1825 from Harmonist religious leader George Rapp in order to establish his utopian communal colony. The social experiment, designed to radically reshape the prevailing social order, lasted a mere two years before dissolving in failure, and has stood as a testimony to the practical non-viability of utopian socialism ever since. The town, however, struggled on, relying upon agriculture, a bit of mining, and the occasional curious tourist to keep the local economy alive. By the 1940s, the Owen family's holdings had dwindled to a single clapboard house where Jane's new husband had spent a hardscrabble Depression-era childhood, often working as a corn husker for a dollar a day.

The house had once been used as a geological laboratory by one of Robert Owen's sons, David Dale Owen, considered to be the father of American geology. David Dale Owen was appointed in 1839 as an official geologist by the U.S. Congress and in that capacity conducted extensive surveys of the American northwest. In Indiana, he discovered that the area surrounding his father's failed social colony was rife with non-catalogued minerals of all description. David Dale Owen also was appointed to serve as Indiana's first state geologist. He has become the patron saint of American geologists and to this day, many still make pilgrimage to the mecca that was David Dale Owen's New Harmony laboratory.

At her Houston high school, Jane had studied the history of New Harmony years before meeting future husband Kenneth. She became inspired by Robert Owen's treatises on social justice and decided early on to work toward the goals that he had so eloquently outlined.

Despite his family's dire financial straits, Kenneth managed to attend college in the 1930s. Upon graduation, he found work as a geologist for

Humble Oil in Houston, working for Jane's father. It wasn't long before Jane became aware that a descendent of Robert Owen was now in the employ of her father's company. Jane and Kenneth connected almost instantly and within a few months they became engaged and set off to Ontario with wedding plans in place.

When the young couple stopped in New Harmony, Kenneth's home-town, en route to Houston after their Canadian honeymoon in 1941, Jane was appalled at the widespread decay and deterioration she encountered. She immediately decided to bring this forsaken flower of America's heritage back into bloom. Thanks in large part to Mrs. Jane's efforts over the ensuing seven decades, New Harmony is today recog-nized as one of Indiana's foremost historic landmark communities and is often compared to Williamsburg, Virginia, as a window into America's past. But there are many who feel that the true "national treas-ure" in New Harmony is Jane Owen herself.

"You see, I don't believe in Utopia at all," she offers, seated beneath the frilled canopy of her environmentally correct electric golf cart as she deftly tools around New Harmony's side streets and byways. "Utopia is not a place. It is a glorious moment—the utopian moment. And if you try to make it a place, then you're bound to be disappointed." This is New Harmony's message to the world, drawn from the gospel accord-ing to Mrs. Jane: Perfection is linked not to place, but rather to time. "Take a beautiful flower," she elaborates. "It blooms and then it shatters. But by blooming, it has achieved perfection." She expresses dismay about today's materialistic society and sniffs at churches that are placing giant TV screens in front of the altar. "They are seeking a material answer to a spiritual need," she says.

Mrs. Jane's passionate expressions about today's consumer culture and societal ills are hardly the harangues of a political dogmatist. Her outspoken opinions about the George W. Bush regime's war in Iraq are tempered by the gentle manner of a lifelong pacifist. "I never thought a military solution was the answer to anything. Not ever. So I count myself as a devout pacifist," she says without a hint of trepidation, "and

I was a pacifist on December 8, 1941, and on September 12, 2001, as well." Enlarging upon that subject, she goes on to recall a visit with Indiana senator Richard Lugar on her 80th birthday in 1995. "He told me we had more to fear from terrorists at home than attacks from abroad and the very next day they blew up the Federal Building in Oklahoma City." While hardly partisan, she believes that Lugar would have been a better president than Bush.

Mrs. Jane's strongest passions emerge when she speaks about her late husband, Kenneth, who passed away in 2002, and his legendary family—a family deeply interwoven into the fabric of American history. "The Owens were hundreds of years ahead of their time," she explains.

Robert Owen's foray into social engineering in America was preceded by copious published essays that expounded on his two overarching principles: the elimination of poverty and the elimination of religion. His lifelong goal was nothing less than a complete makeover of the human race. His devotion to designing the perfect community structure—wherein everything, from personal property to childrearing responsibilities, was shared equally—was matched only by his virulent antipathy toward all formal religions, which he said were "based on the same absurd imagination and which made mankind a weak, imbecilic animal; a furious bigot and fanatic; or a miserable hypocrite."

In 1825, Robert Owen established an experimental community in Orbiston, near Glasgow, Scotland, as well as the one in Harmony, Indiana. After both of Owen's experiments ended in failure, he and his wife returned to London, England. Mrs. Jane speaks about her husband's great-great-grandfather as if she had just had breakfast with him that morning. "Robert was coming up in the world, then he married the daughter of the boss and next he bought the cotton mill," she explains, succinctly summarizing his early life. "But he lost his hold on reality when he came here. He thought he was in heaven. He was a dreamer."

If Robert Owen were to somehow walk the streets of modern-day New Harmony, he would most likely be both delighted and shocked. He would find the simple tree-lined lanes dotted with artists' galleries much to his liking, but he would be totally baffled by the community's many religious retreats and places of meditation and worship. The idyllic artistic and spiritual community that Mrs. Jane has forged in today's New Harmony recently prompted a reporter from the *St. Louis Post Dispatch* to comment: "It appears that Robert Owen's dreams are now finally coming true." While this is certainly the case, the town's many religious sites would more likely give him nightmares.

Mrs. Jane played hostess to the David Dale Owen Geological Conference at the New Harmony laboratory in the summer of 2007, welcoming leading scientists from all corners of the world. "They were like little schoolboys," she says, "running around the lawn saying 'Look over here, it's a trilobite' (a fossilized extinct insect). They were chattering about trilobites in seven different languages. I was so excited it took me days to get over it." But Mrs. Jane sees a larger meaning in events such as the conference. "It's what we're put on earth for: to pool our understanding of the universe— whether it's cancer research or the discovery of the minerals of the earth," she says. "This was a glorious golden moment in the history of our community. It was one of those utopian moments I spoke of that embodies the true spirit of New Harmony."

Mrs. Jane is adept at reciting the Owen family lineage. "Patriarch Robert Owen begat Richard Dale, who begat Horace Pestalozzi Owen, the father of my father-in-law, Richard, who in turn begat my Kenneth." A twinkle comes to her eye as she recalls how Kenneth would tease her and ask: "Who do you think you married, Jane?" And her gleeful reply: "I married all of you. I'm a bigamist! I'm married to the whole Owen family."

Jane's marriage to Kenneth endured for sixty-one years, but not without its share of heartache. Their two daughters fell victim to the polio scourge that swept America in the 1950s. But even this tragedy served to benefit the community to which Jane Owen is so fully committed. "When my children came down with polio, I built a pool, and my little polio-stricken daughters taught the whole neighborhood how to swim," Mrs. Jane says with an audible catch in her voice. "We operate a free swimming program over the summer and today every child in New Harmony who wants to is taught how to swim in that same pool."

Mrs. Jane's educational background prepared her well for her future role as the keeper of the Owen family legacy. During the 1930s, she attended Bryn Mawr College and the Washington School of Diplomacy. Her most profound tutelage took place in 1950 as she studied under the great Christian existential philosopher Paul Tillich at the Union Theological Seminary in New York. Tillich, considered by many as the most influential Protestant theologian of the twentieth century, is memorialized in New Harmony's Tillich Park, thanks to the efforts of Mrs. Jane, who arranged to have her mentor's ashes interred there in 1966.

Mrs. Jane went to work almost immediately upon her arrival in New Harmony in 1941, tilting at the formidable task of rehabilitating the Owen family heritage. The newlyweds were to take up residence at the family's one remaining property, the old laboratory and Kenneth's childhood home. The couple divided their time between Houston, where Kenneth continued his duties at Humble Oil, and New Harmony—a practice Mrs. Jane still observes today.

Mrs. Jane vividly recalls her despair during those first difficult days in New Harmony: "The day we arrived was during an August heat wave—sweltering hot—and we did not even stay at the laboratory, because it was not ready to receive us. So we stayed in a nearby hotel for a while. New Harmony was a dirty little town, dirty with coal soot. It was filthy." But she did not permit dirt or despair to impair her determination. "You simply have to decide what is real in life—the history, the nobility of the people that lived here; you have to look beyond the dirt and the grime."

Her first memorable run-in was with the proprietor of "a little honky-tonk truck stop" across the street from their home who insisted on blaring raucous music all night long and whose patrons regularly dumped their litter on the young couple's front lawn. "I'm the most important thing in this town," the owner told her bluntly. "Oh no, you're not," she corrected him. "Where would you be if the geologists hadn't lived here first? You are the end result of the efforts, the brains and hearts of the people who came here first. You're just a latter-day noisemaker!" She succeeded in getting the truck stop to mend its ways and eventually relocate.

New Harmony, in those days, was little more than a wide spot along a dusty stretch of highway. Having been raised in the select social circles of Houston, adjusting to the rigors of small-town Indiana was not easy for the transplanted debutante. "This was the opposite of Houston. In New Harmony everything had to be earned. Everything had been given to me in Houston—the gated community, the beautiful house, the beautiful everything, the servants, all of that," Mrs. Jane says. But it was amid the soot and solitude of southern Indiana that she found her true calling: "This—the rebuilding of historic New Harmony—is something I can set my heart and treasure to."

It wasn't long before Mrs. Jane came into contact with the provincial racism that characterized that place and time. Her attempt to bring an all-black choir to sing in their church during the couple's first Christmas in New Harmony was met with alarm. "Oh no, my dear, you can't do that," she was told by the church elders. "They'll be tarred and feathered." The shadow of the Ku Klux Klan then extended across the Wabash Valley and easily engulfed any progressive sensibilities that still may have existed in New Harmony.

During the 1960s, Mrs. Jane invited one of the country's greatest African American operatic vocalists to perform in her church. Adele Addison shattered barriers and stereotypes in the musical concert world. Diva Addison had provided Bess's powerful singing voice in the 1959 film version of Porgy and Bess. Despite this and despite the fact that she had been selected by Leonard Bernstein to sing at the opening of Lincoln Center in New York, a contingent of locals had made plans to "keep that n_____ from singing in the church." Mrs. Jane got wind of their intentions and hired several big bruising bouncers to stand guard at the church entry. The beefed-up security protection proved effective and the concert went off smoothly. "She sang so beautifully and her voice just floated out above the walls and into the streets," recalls Mrs. Jane. "We call it an open church and I believe we did open some hearts and minds that day."

But fighting racial intolerance in small town Indiana was more or less a byproduct of Mrs. Jane's primary mission: elevating New Harmony out of the abyss of history into which it had fallen. Accomplishing this one-woman renaissance required resources, however—financial resources. "Out of the goodness of my father's heart and purse, I had the resources with which to begin the job," she explains, "but not enough to finish it. For that I needed help from Lilly." For further financial support, Mrs. Jane turned to the Lilly Endowment, one of the largest philanthropic foundations in the country, established by the family of pharmaceutical company founder Eli Lilly. "I always would pray a lot for help," Mrs. Jane says. "I'm still praying today."

Prayer? A quick tour of today's New Harmony—the restoration of atheist Robert Owen's experimental community—reveals it to be a haven for religious tolerance and faith-based understanding. In Tillich Park, for example, one finds Tillich's engraved message that reads: "Man and nature belong together in their created glory, in their tragedy, and in their salvation."

According to Mrs. Jane, mankind is today experiencing a tragedy of nature. She readily bemoans the greed and the squandering of natural resources by the U.S. government and, despite her Exxon-ic bloodlines, she feels that exploitation by large corporations has taken its toll on nature. Jane Owen has spent the better part of her long life as a savior of nature. She continues to preserve the natural beauty, as well as the history of New Harmony, while making sure it continues to provide a spiritual and intellectual refuge for artists, writers, and educators. "I am passionate about New Harmony," she proclaims. "I'm like a bride coming back to her beloved each time I return."

Strolling the well-manicured streets of today's New Harmony or touring the town's many historic sites via fringe-topped golf cart, it's hard to imagine the backwater bog that greeted the newlywed Jane back in the 1940s. From the rustic New Harmony Inn to the futuristically dramatic Atheneum and the renowned Roofless Church, the town attracts thousands of visitors each year. New Harmony is studded with shrines, classic statuary, and artistic retreats designed to permit spiritual meditation. One of the area's most outstanding attractions is the Jane Blaffer and Kenneth Dale Owen Recreational Trail, which winds along the riparian area between forks of the Wabash River, rich with pathways, unique flora, lush greenways, and numerous historic sites.

The cost of developing and maintaining this historic and cultural oasis obviously cannot be borne solely by the county tax base. "I lose $2 million a year on this project, because I keep it looking like a country club, manicured flowers and the like," Mrs. Jane says. "But no dues," she is quick to add, her populist sensibilities coming to the fore. "I hate real country clubs. I really loathe them. They're exclusive. They say: 'You're not good enough, we don't think you have enough money or enough class.'" And class is one thing she unquestionably under-stands—and embodies. To this day, Mrs. Jane enjoys a well-earned rep-utation as a devoted social activist and crusader.

The years and decades simply disappear in her presence, transcend-ing history and creating an energy field where yesterday could just as easily be 24 hours or 240 years ago. When discussing her anti-war—or more correctly, pro-peace—principles, her sentiments could just as like-ly be drawn from Tom Paine as from Tom Hayden: "Wars start in cap-ital cities, not in little towns," she says. "Every war that you can think of began in a capital of a country. I wanted to have an impact if I could, on our nation's capital in Washington. But I was not allowed. They were determined to go into Korea, they were determined to go into Vietnam. In the 1940s, I wanted to put the peace statue by Jacques Lipchitz on display in Washington, but they would not allow it."

This bronze statue of a welcoming Madonna inside a tear-shaped canopy is titled "The Descent of the Holy Spirit." It is today housed at New Harmony's Roofless Church, designed by famed architect Phillip Johnson. The statue's ecumenical inscription reads: "Jacob Lipchitz, Jew, faithful to the faith of his ancestors, has made this virgin for the good will of all mankind that the spirit might prevail."

"The statue might not have slowed them down," Mrs. Jane says, "but it would have helped me—the fact that I injected a little drop of sanity into Washington, D.C. That would have done my heart some good, if nothing more."

The disappointment of that effort is as vivid to Mrs. Jane as if she had attempted it during the war in Iraq instead of shortly after World War II, some sixty-odd years before. Her dominion stretches across the centuries as well. For example, Mrs. Jane is not the least bit abashed about discussing her nocturnal discussions with various historical figures.

"The other night I dreamt that George had come back," she reveals. George? "I've always been so enamored of George Washington and his colleagues." Oh, that George. "And he came on a white horse in the middle of the night. I said to him: 'George, hurry! You saved us once. Now you must save us again!'" She goes on to explain that she has admired Washington since she learned that he refused to move his troops to better protect his own home at Mt. Vernon, opting to seize a minor strategic advantage instead. "'Let them burn it,' he said. 'I'm not moving the troops from over here to there. The troops need to be here.' He was selfless," Mrs. Jane enthuses. "He was not thinking of what was good for George, but what was good for the country."

Mrs. Jane believes with all her heart that New Harmony has a lesson for all of America. Like Washington, Robert Owen was selfless and arrived generously, with hands wide open, ready to do what was good for the community, not only for himself. The idealists who established the New Harmony colony brought with them the culture and intellect of the Old World. Like a certain young bride, they arrived at New Harmony with what she calls "well-furnished minds."

It is through her dedication and tireless efforts to promote and enhance New Harmony, a touchstone for Indiana's legacy of largesse, that Mrs. Jane can easily be seen to have a well-furnished heart as well. "It's not what's in it for me, but what's in it for America," she says in a characteristic posture of determination. "I was so moved by the story of these people in my youth and I'm still moved by them. Even to this very day."

Making sure that the New Harmony story endures and survives her own lifespan is the mission of what has become Mrs. Jane's most vital endeavor: the New Harmony Project. Inaugurated in 1987, this two-week annual retreat is designed to nurture members of the creative community such as authors, playwrights, and screenwriters who offer hope and celebrate the dignity of the human spirit. Over the past two decades, hundreds of actors, directors, dramatists, and others have developed more than 140 scripts for the stage and screenplays at the retreat. Through projects such as this one, Mrs. Jane has ensured her own legacy as New Harmony's cultural guardian angel.

It was in recognition of her support for such projects and in appreciation of her lifelong dedication to preserving and enhancing Indiana's well-known landmark community that, in 2007, Indiana governor Mitch Daniels awarded Mrs. Jane the state's highest tribute, the Sachem Award. Only the third Hoosier in history to have been thus honored, Mrs. Jane joined legendary UCLA basketball coach John Wooden and former Notre Dame University president Reverend Theodore Hesburgh in the rarefied pantheon of Indiana's most outstanding achievers.

As any visitor to New Harmony will attest, it is a unique place. Nurtured by the gentle hand of Jane Blaffer Owen, it is a place that will benefit generations to come. In what may be described as a showcase for humanity's better nature, New Harmony's every stone and stair step bear the imprint of Kenneth Dale Owen's buckwheat bride.

Ernestine Raclin

First Lady of South Bend

I learned everything I needed to know about business on the back of a horse." With that, Ernestine Raclin straightens her petite frame and begins to talk about her teenage years and the lessons she learned from her father. Dressed in a smart black business suit accented with a gold chain and matching earrings, she looks like anything but the horsewoman she described. An attractive woman with soft gray hair and hazel eyes, Raclin has a ready smile and a robust laugh. When she extends her hand, it is small and delicate, belying her personality. This woman—all five feet of her—is one of the most influential people in South Bend, Indiana.

Known to her friends as Ernie, Raclin admits to growing up a daddy's girl, and with good reason. Her father, Ernest Melvin Morris, was a self-made man. His mother died in 1896, when he was barely a teenager, and he was abandoned by his father not long after. Morris lived in the town of Teegarden, Indiana, a half-day buggy ride south of South Bend. To survive, he worked odd jobs from house to house, often sleeping in his employer's stable.

Morris was bright and self-confident. It was the dawn of the twentieth century and he knew his ticket to a better life was an education. He intended to be a lawyer. He attended Valparaiso University between periods of employment and passed sufficient equivalency tests to graduate in less than two years. Still short on money, he postponed law

school and found work in South Bend as the only teacher in a one-room schoolhouse. When Indiana adopted regulations requiring that music be taught in every school, Morris could not continue because he lacked the ability to teach music.

His desire to become an attorney led Morris and his horse, Dexter, to the University of Notre Dame, where he convinced an impressed President John Cavanaugh to grant him a partial scholarship to the law school. Dexter got a free ride, including unlimited oats and a place to sleep in the stable. Morris graduated with honors in one year.

In 1913, Morris married Ella Keen, a teacher from Cincinnati who at 5' was a foot shorter than her husband. Ernie not only inherited her mother's physical stature, but also her concern for the plight of those less fortunate. Ella Keen Morris was active in social-service organizations and was the first woman school board member in Indiana. She also established the South Bend Symphony, an institution for which her daughter served as president in 2002.

The Morrises were poor but like many young people of that era, they saw promise and opportunity. They were ambitious. While practicing law, Morris formed a group of associates to invest together in real estate. When it became apparent that returns from this activity would not be significant, Morris had an alternative vision. Henry Ford was manufacturing his Model "T" automobile, and many potential buyers wanted to own this transportation miracle. In the beginning, these "Tin Lizzies" sold for almost $1,000. Later, because of savings from mass production, the price dropped to a few hundred dollars—or about $4,000 in today's dollars. Residents of South Bend, most of whom were tied to the agricultural economy, couldn't afford to pay even that amount all at once. Looking for an alternative to real estate investments, the Morris-led Associates Corporation made it possible for automobile dealers to finance their customers' purchases. A new business was born.

Morris devoted himself to the new company. "My father worked around the clock often spending nights and weekends at the office," Raclin recalls. Associates Corp. was among the first companies of its kind, and the risk paid off handsomely. Between 1908 and 1927, Ford built fifteen million automobiles with the Model T engines, and most of those purchased on credit were financed at Associates or similar companies that sprang up around the country. The company prospered due to Morris's determination and work ethic and expanded very quickly to customer loans and insurance sales. By the early 1940s, the Morrises were safely ensconced in the upper middle class.

Raclin was born on October 25, 1927, as Ernestine Marilyn Morris. She later changed her name to Ernestine Melvin Morris in honor of her father. Her only sibling, Mary Lou, was eleven years older and already had moved out of the home by the time Ernie reached her teenage years. With Mary Lou gone, Ernie was essentially an only child doted on by her mother and father. Because Ernie suffered from amblyopia, a disorder commonly known as lazy eye, she had to undergo many surgeries; normal sports were impossible. "Because I saw two of everything I couldn't do anything such as hit a tennis ball," she said. The doctor suggested that she exercise in some other manner in order to increase her physical stamina and bolster her confidence. Her father loved to ride horses and although Dexter was gone by this time, Morris purchased and stabled horses so that he and Ernie could ride together. They enjoyed the horses and each other's company at least twice a week for years. Ernie became a seasoned horsewoman who won many ribbons showing and jumping the family's horses, even winning a national championship.

The exercise served its purpose. Ernie developed into a confident young woman and perhaps more importantly, those rides with her father gave her the business savvy she would need in later years. "Dad would always use a case study approach in talking to me about different challenges he had in business to see what I thought. It was a wonderful time to just be together," she says. Genuinely interested in his daughter's point of view, Morris had complete confidence in her on and off the horse.

The summer of 1942, Ernie arose each day at the first sign of light to assist the trainer with her family's horses before reporting to work at

Associates, where she continued to learn from her father. That summer she met an older man who would dramatically change her life. At the time, the U.S. Navy conducted midshipman classes at Notre Dame and the community sponsored "Tea Dances" to support these young men while in training. While attending such a dance with an acquaintance, Ernie met midshipman Oliver Cromwell Carmichael Jr. He was immediately smitten by this precocious young lady, who had yet to turn 15. "He was very much a southern gentleman," Ernie recalls.

Carmichael, known as Mike, was already a graduate of Vanderbilt University and Duke University School of Law. Instead of asking Ernie her age, he asked what year she was in school and misunderstood her answer. Mike thought she was a college sophomore, but she was still in high school. Their romance blossomed nevertheless, and Ernie soon began her prep school education at Ward Belmont School in Nashville, Tennessee. Since Ward Belmont was associated with a college of similar name, Ernie could continue the age charade. While she finished prep school, Mike was at war serving as commander aboard a submarine chaser in the Solomon Islands. Ernie continued her deception for four years—or so she thought. Although she did not know it until much later, her mother had told Mike's mother her true age and status in school. When Ernie finally confessed to Mike in a letter that took many hours to compose, he surprised her by admitting that he had known all along. Ernie became Ernestine Carmichael in the fall of 1946 at age 18.

After a brief sojourn in South Bend, where Mike worked in the legal department at Associates, the young couple moved to New York. Mike studied public law and government at Columbia University, eventually earning a master's degree and Ph.D.

In 1951, Ernie was crushed by the death of her father. Thoughts of moving back to South Bend, however, gave way to support of Mike's budding academic career and to starting their family. After graduation Mike secured a position as dean of students at Vanderbilt University, where his father had been chancellor. He also became the first executive director of the Vanderbilt University Foundation. In 1956, Mike was named president of Converse College in Spartanburg, South Carolina. Ernie enjoyed campus life and was excited by her role as the wife of a college president. She was actively involved in both the college and its host community when fate intervened.

After Ernie's father died, her brother-in-law, Robert Oare, had been named chairman of Associates. On a snowy day in March 1960, a Northwest Airlines flight bound for Miami exploded and crashed in a farmer's field near Tell City, Indiana, killing all onboard, including Oare. Mike, who was a member of the Associates board of directors, was summoned home to run the company. The couple moved back to South Bend, where Ernie honed her career as a community volunteer and leader even as she raised their four children: daughters Carmine (Carmi) and Ernestine (Tina) and sons Oliver (Crom) and Stanley (Clark).

During the next ten years, Ernie distinguished herself as a community servant and quietly began to assume leadership roles. She was asked to chair the United Way fundraising campaign in South Bend in the early 1970s, a position no woman had previously held. Aware that no campaign could succeed in South Bend without the cooperation of organized labor, she sought advice from the chairman of the AFL-CIO union and was told, "A woman cannot do this job." So she declined, serving instead as vice chair, a position the union chairman thought was more suitable for a woman. She succeeded so well that the next year— with the union leader's blessing—she was asked to chair the campaign and became the first woman in the United States to lead a local United Way campaign. To no one's surprise, it was a record year. Ernie's efforts on behalf of the United Way were so outstanding that she was tapped to serve on the United Way of America's national board of governors, the first woman to do so.

Her fundraising experience also helped Ernie repay Notre Dame for the kindness shown to her father. Mike Carmichael chaired the 1968 Summa campaign that raised more than $60 million for the school, and in 1976 Ernie became the first woman to lead a University of Notre Dame fund drive, the Campaign for Notre Dame, raising $150 million.

Although she never graduated from college, she was named the school's first female trustee in 1976. In recognition of her dedication and her achievements, the university awarded Ernie an honorary Doctor of Laws degree in 1978.

Ernie led such fundraising campaigns by example. Her charitable giving has focused primarily on education, arts, and her community. The University of Notre Dame has been a beneficiary over the years. Contributions included support for a university gallery at South Bend's Center for History. That gallery, named for her, features exhibitions about Notre Dame's history. Ernie also has been a tireless supporter of St. Mary's College, which awarded her an honorary doctorate. In addition, Ernie has been a major benefactor of Indiana University South Bend, where the School of the Arts now carries her name, as does Ivy Tech's Culinary Arts Program. More recently, Ernie, along with her daughter Carmi and son-in-law Christopher J. Murphy III and the family's Carmichael Foundation, helped fund construction of an IU School of Medicine–South Bend research and educational center on the Notre Dame campus, which is used by both universities. The Ernestine Raclin and O.C. Carmichael Hall was dedicated on Ernie's 78th birthday in 2005.

The family's philanthropy was fueled by Ernest Morris's business acumen, which has been passed along through the generations. Associates Corp. was just the beginning. In 1963, Associates acquired the First Bank and Trust Company, a bank Morris had been instrumental in establishing more than thirty years before. Three years after Associates was sold to Gulf and Western Industries, the family in 1971 joined other former shareholders to repurchase the bank. First Bank and Trust Bank Co. became a freestanding publicly owned company named FBT Bancorp. The bank and holding company names were changed to 1st Source in 1981. The family still owns about 30 percent of the holding company's stock.

Although Ernie had made a name for herself as a leader in the charitable world, she did not demonstrate her business savvy until tragedy again struck the family in 1976. Her husband Mike suffered a fatal heart attack on the tennis court as he was delivering an overhead smash. He was 56.

In deference to the size of the family holdings and out of respect for her competency and leadership in charitable activities, Ernie was tapped to chair the bank's board. She was not on the board or employed by the bank at that time, but the confidence she had acquired as a young girl had not waned. She accepted the position with the thought that "nobody watches your investment better than you do."

Ernie undertook this new role with full commitment. Her father's work ethic was not lost on her. She balanced the careers of mother, volunteer, leader, and business executive smoothly but not without sacrifice. She reluctantly resigned from many of her volunteer positions. Working became her hobby. She slept only four or five hours a night. During Ernie's tenure, the hallmark of the bank was personal contact and customer service. She called on customers personally with positive results. Companies and individuals appreciated the overtures of this determined executive. When Ernie took the reins at 1st Source Bank, the institution had assets of $331 million and an annual net income of $1.9 million. In 2007, 1st Source was the third-largest banking company headquartered in Indiana, with assets of about $4.5 billion and annual income of more than $30 million.

Ernie's success was noticed. She was invited to serve on the board of other banks, including in 1979 First Chicago Corp. and its subsidiary, The First National Bank of Chicago, the nation's fifth largest bank. She was the first woman to serve in that capacity.

Ernie sought assistance in the family business from eldest daughter Carmi's husband, Chris Murphy, a lawyer and banker with Citibank. He joined 1st Source in 1977 and shortly thereafter became its president and CEO. Murphy had earned a bachelor's degree in government and international relations from Notre Dame, a law degree from the University of Virginia, and an MBA with distinction from Harvard University. He was elected to chair the holding company and bank board upon Ernie's retirement in 1998. In a fitting tribute to Ernie that exemplifies her distinct accomplishments, 1st Source Bank in 1999 established the Ernestine M. Raclin Community Leadership Award to honor and encourage those who give of themselves to benefit others. The award is given annually to as many as five 1st Source employees and five employees of locally owned companies in communities the bank serves.

Now serving as chairman emeritus of 1st Source Corp. and 1st Source Bank, Ernie still comes to the office most days, continuing her role as a community leader.

Retirement gave her more time to spend with her second husband, Robert L. Raclin, whom she married a little over a year after Mike's death. Bob, who was head of commodities trading for Paine Webber in Chicago, met Ernie when they were fixed up by mutual friends. "He called and asked to meet me at the Drake Hotel in Chicago. I had very short hair at the time. I said, 'How will I know you?' He said, 'I have gray hair and a marine crew cut.' And he said, 'How will I know you?' I said, 'I have gray hair and a marine crew cut,'" she recalls. "Later he told me that right then he had fallen in love with me."

For many years, they had what she refers to as a marriage of inconvenience—with Bob living in Chicago and Ernie in South Bend. They met each weekend in one city or the other for eighteen years. After a short stint as Undersecretary of Health and Human Services in Washington, D.C., Bob finally retired and moved to South Bend. He died in 2008 at the age of 89.

Education has been an important focus of Raclin's philanthropic endeavors. In addition to her work in South Bend, she is a former trustee of Converse College in South Carolina and a board member of the Indiana University Foundation. She also has served on the Purdue University President's Council and the Independent Colleges of Indiana board of directors.

Other areas of emphasis include arts and the community. She is past president of the Indiana University Arts Foundation of South Bend. "In order to have a really well-rounded community with true quality of life, you need an active arts program that is evident throughout the area," Raclin says. In 1999, IU South Bend presented her with an honorary Doctor of Law and in 2006 the Chancellor's Medal. She was the first woman to chair its advisory board.

As for community, Raclin is a former chair of Project Future, a not-for-profit economic development organization she co-founded in 1982. She also led its first campaign, which raised more than $5 million. Project Future works to enhance the economic development of South Bend, Mishawaka, and St. Joseph County. In the past twenty years, Project Future has played a role in attracting and sustaining more than a billion dollars in capital investments in St. Joseph County.

Through the Carmichael Foundation and personally, Raclin supports countless other causes throughout the region. Many buildings bear the family name, including the Morris Inn at Notre Dame and the Morris Civic Auditorium in downtown South Bend. Despite her many "firsts"—she was the first woman on the board of directors for the South Bend and state Chambers of Commerce as well as NIPSCO Industries Inc., Northern Indiana Public Service Co., MidCon Corp., and People's Energy Corp.—Raclin insists gender has never been an issue for her.

She advises young people to work and study hard. "Do not be afraid of hard work. Have a deep faith but don't wear your religion on your sleeve. If you make a mistake, get up and do the job again and do it better the next time."

Well-earned honors continue to be bestowed upon Raclin for her distinguished career in business and her devotion to her community. In 2001, she received the Henry A. Russo Medal for lifetime achievement in ethical fundraising, presented by the Center on Philanthropy at Indiana University.

Of Raclin's numerous awards and recognitions—including eight honorary degrees—perhaps none is more moving than the E.M. Morris Award conferred in 1977 by the IU South Bend School of Business and Economics. Named for her father, the award is given to leaders who advance business and quality of life. It was a fitting tribute to Ernie and her father, who recognized her enormous potential for leadership and taught her what she needed to know to achieve it—all from the back of a horse. He would have been proud.

Nancy Shepherd Fitzgerald

A Champion On and Off the Course

ancy Fitzgerald's view of God was tragically formed when she was 5 years old, and it took nearly three decades for her to change her perspective. During her childhood in the 1940s and 1950s, her family spent summers at a cottage on Gall Lake in western Michigan. Young Nancy and her sister Carole were in the yard at the cottage playing croquet one day when their babysitter lost track of 2-year-old Stephen. During the search for her brother, Nancy walked to the dock and found him face down in the water. "I remember at that point asking God to save Stephen," she said. "I believed God could do that if He really wanted to." But when Stephen drowned anyway, she questioned the existence of a God that would allow an innocent child to die.

That doubt endured well into adulthood. Fitzgerald was a wife, mother, and golf champion living in Carmel, Indiana, when she next looked for God—twenty-seven years after her brother's death. A friend shared with her his newly found belief in Jesus Christ and suggested she read the gospel of John in the New Testament. So when she left Carmel for a golf outing in Florida, she took a Bible and her friend's advice. The reading opened her eyes to the possibility that God existed and that—

in spite of all the pain she still vividly recalled—God's love and faithfulness was a reality she had simply denied.

That trip launched Fitzgerald on an intensive investigation into the reliability of the scriptures, studying the Bible and the writings of Francis Schaffer, an evangelical Christian theologian. She searched out mentors such as Christian author Josh McDowell, Prison Ministries founder Chuck Colson, and Dr. David Noble of Summit Ministries. "I came to an understanding of God that eliminated a lot of the doubts that I had harbored all those earlier years," Fitzgerald says. "The truth of the Bible and Jesus were verifiable."

Not content to have just her own spiritual questions answered, Fitzgerald wanted to share her newfound convictions with others. "I had a passion for working with kids, especially teenagers. I know the struggles they face, especially after high school when they leave home and are trying to find themselves apart from their families," she explained. So in 2005, Fitzgerald established Anchors Away Inc., a not-for-profit organization that has grown from an informal weekly gathering of high school students in her Carmel home to a published curriculum studied in all fifty states and twelve foreign countries.

Given the zeal that has enabled her to develop Anchors Away into an international ministry, it is clear that Fitzgerald has her fair share of enthusiasm. It was that kind of focused dedication that helped her excel at her first passion—the challenging game of golf.

★ ★ ★

Nancy Shepherd was born October 18, 1943, and made what seemed to her family the natural transition from "cradle to bunker." "When I was 4 years old, my father literally placed me in sand bunkers and I would make sand castles while he practiced his chipping," she recalls. Her father, Joel, was an amateur golf champion eventually inducted into the Michigan Golf Hall of Fame. When Nancy lost interest in sand castles, she "caddied" for her father in several tournaments, occasionally riding on the pull-cart. By age 7, she was playing golf herself. She entered her first tournament at 10.

Joel and his wife, Suzanne, were civic-minded citizens involved in several community organizations in their hometown of Kalamazoo, Michigan. Joel was a staunch Republican, Suzanne a fervent Democrat. Together, they raised four successful children. In addition to Nancy, there's older brother Joel, who played golf at the University of Texas and operates Shepherd Specialty Paper in Kalamazoo; younger brother Earl, who owns Seattle-based National Shelter Products; and sister Carole Birch, a social worker in Parchment, Michigan.

Nancy's mother was a community volunteer recognized as Michigan's "Woman of the Year" for her civic contributions to the city of Kalamazoo. Her father owned and operated Shepherd Fuel Co. before establishing Shepherd Products Company to produce home-building materials. "My father was extremely encouraging and taught me a great deal about golf and life," Fitzgerald says. "He was an outstanding golfer and businessman who made more business deals on the golf course than I could ever dream."

He also taught there. Before 10-year-old Nancy's first tournament began, her father bought her a new set of golf clubs and took her out to practice. "I was such a brat," she recalls. "After my first stroke with my 3-iron, I threw the club because I had hit the ball badly. My father picked up the iron and put it in his bag. The same thing happened with my 5-iron, 9-iron, and wedge. I threw them all after hitting bad shots. Each time, my father picked up the tossed club and calmly placed it in his own golf bag." After finishing the round, her father delivered the bad news: He was going to keep the clubs Nancy had thrown until she realized that her behavior and character were more important than her win-loss record. "I was devastated, but head-strong," Fitzgerald recalls. Still, "the next day I played my first tournament with just my putter, 7-iron, and a driver and I still won!"

The winning never stopped. With her father as her coach, she captured numerous junior events and won golf tournaments all over the state of Michigan, including the Kalamazoo City Championship.

Although high schools did not offer girls' varsity sports at the time,

Nancy played intramural sports and practiced golf with the boys' team. After graduating in 1961, she had her sights set on attending the University of Colorado in order to pursue another sports passion—skiing. "My father soon surmised that I would not get much studying done if I went to Colorado, so he took me to Indiana University to visit the campus," Fitzgerald says. "He had graduated from Wabash College in the late 1930s, so he was familiar with Indiana. . . . I fell in love with it."

She majored in education and became especially interested in studying gifted students and those with developmental disorders. During summers, she worked at the Shakespeare Rod and Fly Company in Kalamazoo, where the owner allowed her time off to play in golf tournaments. While at IU, she continued to play golf. Although the school did not have a women's team, she played in tournaments on her own. She qualified for the National Collegiate Athletic Association's golf tournament in 1965. Nancy earned a bachelor's degree in education from IU in 1966 and master's degrees in health sciences and education the following year. Her master's thesis explored the notion of integrating special-needs children into regular classes.

During her senior year, she met the man she would marry: Edward Fitzgerald, now a retired heart surgeon. Although both attended IU, they were introduced during spring break in Fort Lauderdale, Florida. They married later that year. When Ed graduated from the IU School of Medicine in 1968, the couple moved to Pennsylvania, where he had accepted a residency position at the Hershey Medical Center.

During the years they lived in Hershey, Nancy Fitzgerald began to realize just how good she could be on the links. She worked as a substitute teacher so she could be free to play in golf tournaments when needed. She pursued perfection with the passion that would define her life, winning the Harrisburg Woman's District Golf Tournament twice and competing in a few professional tournaments. Despite qualifying and playing in the pro contests, she opted to retain her amateur status by refusing prize money. Nonetheless, Fitzgerald competed against the top women golfers in the country. In 1969, she traveled throughout the

United States competing in national amateur tournaments. But competing at the highest level was not without its challenges.

"By the end of 1969, I was exhausted," she recalls. "It was very tiring to travel across the country and sleep in hotels. Golf wasn't fun anymore. I felt I could compete at the professional level, but I just didn't want to. I decided I wanted to be a mother. For me, being on the national golf circuit was not conducive to a healthy family life."

Fitzgerald didn't give up the sport, however. Rather, she simply redirected her efforts to state and local tournaments—still highly competitive—and continued to dominate. In 1974, Fitzgerald and her husband moved their young family from Pennsylvania to Carmel, Indiana, where Ed became a thoracic surgeon with a cardiology group affiliated with St. Vincent Hospital. Nancy continued to golf, even as she raised four children: Scott, Mark, Andrew, and Kelly.

Over the next several years, Fitzgerald became an eleven-time Indianapolis Women's City Champion and eight-time medalist. She won the Crooked Stick Country Club's Women's Invitational three times and still holds the women's course record of 66. At the state level, Fitzgerald won the Indiana Women's State Golf Championship five times in four different decades (1978, 1981, 1992, 2004, and 2006). She also is a seven-time winner of the Hunting Creek Invitational in Kentucky and a seven-time Indiana State Mid-Amateur Champion. In seven different years, she was selected to represent Indiana at the U.S. Golf Association Team Championships.

Fitzgerald recalls that in the 1960s and 1970s, women's golf was widely respected, as evidenced by large crowds for local as well as national tournaments. But the spectator climate has changed, likely because golf enthusiasts are either too busy playing themselves or watch national tournaments on television. Plus, it is more difficult to follow local tournaments, since the media don't pay them as much attention as they once did. "In the past, the media did a great job of covering local events. It used to make the headlines for an amateur woman winning a tournament. Now you might read about it in the box scores on the last page. Amateur women tournament golfers can and do play incredible golf and are fun to watch. There is an amazing camaraderie among golfers, creating wonderful friendships that often last for a lifetime. The focus for most amateur golfers is to practice, play well, and spend time with and meet new friends. They celebrate golf for the game and those who play."

Indeed, Fitzgerald said there have been positive developments in the game. In the early years, many clubs didn't embrace women's golf, considering the female players to be a nuisance to men who sought prime tee times to conduct business or as a recreational outlet. Fitzgerald finds that today, for the most part, golfers respect one another no matter their age or gender.

During the years that Fitzgerald was winning local and state tournaments, she also continued to compete at the national level. In 1989, she won the National Club Ladies Championship. In 1994, she tied for first place in the USGA Women's Senior Championship, losing in an 18-hole playoff. Three years later, in 1997, she captured the title. In 1995, 1997, and 1998, she won the Senior Women's Trans-Mississippi Title. In 1996, 1997, and 1998, she won the Canadian Woman's Senior Open Championship. Fitzgerald has been inducted into the Indiana Golf Hall of Fame and the Kalamazoo, Michigan, Golf Hall of Fame. Few women have dominated a sport for so long. She has had three holes in one and considers her greatest win to be the USGA Senior Woman's Championship in 1997.

"It stands out not only for the importance of winning a national championship, but also that I had, for the first time, a game plan as to how I was going to play the last three holes no matter what the score. I stuck to it and won," Fitzgerald explains. "On the 18th hole, the match was tied. I hit a 3-wood off the tee on the par five and laid up with a 5-iron, giving me a full wedge shot to the green instead of a half wedge, which is easier to hit. It worked and I won. I continue to use that strategy as it averts emotional choices in times of stress."

Despite her phenomenal success, Fitzgerald is philosophical about her life playing golf and puts it into perspective. "If you visit our house, the trophies are stuck in a room in the basement. I played the game for the love of it, not for the accolades," she says. "Golf allows you to meet so many people. It is a gift to be able to travel around the world and to have almost an instant connection when you meet someone with a common interest in the sport."

She has especially enjoyed watching younger women enter the game. She notes that young women today can receive scholarships to play at the collegiate level and have the opportunity to travel in a way that was much more difficult when she was their age. "I'm older than most of their parents, but I still love playing with these kids," she enthuses.

If Fitzgerald's résumé ended with her accomplishments on the golf course, it would be lengthy and distinguished. However, her life's story is far more than about driving, chipping, and putting golf balls.

Another of her many accomplishments is founding the Indiana Family Institute, a not-for-profit organization that seeks to strengthen marriage and support families. The nonpartisan group's work is centered on public policy, research, and education related to the health and well-being of Hoosier families. One important initiative has been to encourage ministers, prior to marrying couples, to provide counseling and to promote marriage-enrichment programs. The institute has raised awareness about the importance of reducing single-parenting and the financial, social, and familial hardships that commonly result from not having both a father and mother in a child's life.

Fitzgerald was inspired to start the organization in 1991 after meeting Dr. James Dobson of Focus on the Family, a Christian ministry. She and her husband had attended a Focus on the Family conference in Montana the previous year, and Dobson shared his vision of having education and research organizations in each state to focus on the well-being of families. "How could I have refused that?" she asks.

It is clear that family is indeed an important part of her life. In addition to raising their four children and doting on their three grandchildren, the Fitzgeralds sponsored two children from Vietnam. In the mid-1990s, they took in teenagers Timmy and Jimmy Luu. Timmy, a graduate of ITT, works in heating and air conditioning; Jimmy graduated from IUPUI with a degree in computer science. Their other children all live and work in Denver, Colorado, after being introduced to the scenic western state through annual family ski trips when they were young. Scott is married and owns a tree company; Mark is an orthopedic surgeon; Andrew, a graduate of Indiana University law school, is an attorney; and their daughter, Kelly, like Mark, is a graduate of the Indiana University School of Medicine. She is training to be a pediatric anesthesiologist.

Fitzgerald also has found time to get involved in the community. She is a past president of the Agape Therapeutic Riding Center in Cicero, Indiana, which provides therapeutic horseback riding for special needs children. And she was a member of the board of directors for the Heartland Film Festival, which has gained a national reputation for recognizing and supporting uplifting, life-affirming motion pictures.

But the initiative Fitzgerald is most proud of is Anchors Away, the wide-reaching curriculum that resulted from her own spiritual journey. The program is designed to give young people the guidance, support, and moral training they need to confront the world after they leave home. She cites statistics from studies by the likes of Christian writer and evangelist Josh McDowell, which found that nearly 90 percent of teenagers who regularly attend church while in high school do not do so once they have graduated. Further, only 2 percent can defend what they believe about God and Jesus Christ.

Fitzgerald adopted the name Anchors Away from the naval term "anchors aweigh." One meaning of the term "weigh" is "to heave, hoist or rise up." Thus, when a boat's last anchor is aweigh, it is pulled up from the ocean floor, allowing a ship to set sail and begin navigating toward its destination. The same concept applies to young people—as they are freed from their familial anchors, they can begin their own spiritual journey with direction and purpose.

The Fitzgeralds began holding Sunday evening gatherings for teenagers in their large Carmel home twenty years ago, when their oldest son, Scott, was 17. The tradition continued with their other children, and by the late 1990s, more than 150 high school students were attending the weekly spiritual meetings. "I knew that I had a study course that was special when

I saw how eager these teenagers were to come to our house on Sunday evenings for learning through discussion and reflection," Fitzgerald says. "Part of their reason for coming was social, but they also had a thirst for greater understanding and knowledge."

In order to allow others to replicate the experience, Fitzgerald developed a curriculum of manuals, videotapes, and DVDs that are used by trained teachers and facilitators. Every student of the Anchors Away curriculum studies eight core classes, from Who Is God? and Is the Bible Reliable? to What Is the Trinity? and What Is a Christian and Am I One? Optional courses include a basic introduction to Islam and Judaism and an examination into other life questions such as "Why does God allow suffering?"—something that could have benefited young Nancy in her formative years. Students who successfully complete the Anchors Away curriculum are eligible to receive three hours of college credit through Crossroads Bible College in Indianapolis.

Fitzgerald has taken her study of God and His meaning to humankind even further—writing a book entitled *What God?* that is designed to equip believers and nonbelievers with a practical approach to understanding the foundations of Christianity. She said the book delivers a loving, informative, and nonjudgmental message of truth as it attempts to answer many questions about life, purpose, and hope. It is intended for a wide-ranging audience—individuals searching for answers to questions they have about God, purpose, suffering, hope, and death. The book discusses how Fitzgerald found God and the scriptures to be the truth. It also describes how many of her former students have lived out their faith on a college campus and beyond. She hopes the book will lead readers to develop a faith in Jesus Christ that works in a world that often rejects God and truth.

Whether on the golf course or before teenagers sharing her own faith, Fitzgerald is passionate about using the talents she has been given. She also has also encouraged others to find and use their own talents to confront life's most challenging questions.

Carolyn Y. Woo

☆

Breaking the Mold

*I*n April 2006, U.S. president George W. Bush invited an exclusive group of national leaders to a White House lunch with Hu Jintao, president of China. The guest list included United Nations ambassador John R. Bolton, former U.S. secretary of state Henry Kissinger, and U.S. vice president Dick Cheney. An American woman of Chinese descent was among the assembled elite, undoubtedly chosen for this honor by virtue of her extraordinary achievements in the field of education. Her two cultures, Chinese, which she left many years ago but did not abandon, and American, which she embraced with grace and perfection, came together at lunch with the presidents of two great nations. It was only fitting that Carolyn Y. Woo be included in this occasion.

★ ★ ★

Woo was the product of an unlikely union. Her father, Woo Ching Chee, was a Chinese man who as a young adult embraced the Western culture and assumed the name Peter Woo. He was educated as a marine engineer and naval architect at the Royal Institute of Technology in Glasgow, Scotland, during the pre–World War II years. Unable to attend graduate school because of the turmoil created in Europe during the war, he moved to Hong Kong in 1941 to find work in the ports. About six months later, the island nation fell to the Japanese, who attempted to

press him into service to repair ships. He refused to work for the Japanese and fled to mainland China with a new wife he hardly knew.

Woo's mother, Hung U Lan, was born into a wealthy family and was raised in a strict traditional Chinese environment. She was not sent to school with other children. Instead, she had a tutor and three maids who buffered her from all pressures and took care of her every need. "My mother was raised in the greenhouse," observes Woo. Her mother had escaped to Hong Kong in 1937 as the Japanese invaded China. She returned to the mainland with her husband in 1942.

The marriage of Woo's parents was semi-arranged. They did not know each other well and had only a few unsupervised dates before the marriage was deemed appropriate. Their early years in China were difficult; they moved often to evade the Chinese authorities even as they started their family. After the war, the young couple returned to Hong Kong, a less repressive environment more suitable to Peter Woo's lifestyle. In 1949 they visited mainland China in the hope of finding a life in the country of their birth, but returned discouraged by the imminent Communist takeover. They would stay in Hong Kong, even though it meant leaving behind most of their assets. Woo's mother was plunged into a society for which she was ill-prepared. She faced adult life and motherhood without her accustomed level of support in a fast-paced modern world. Hong Kong was emerging as a center of opportunity. The streets were alive with activity that to her seemed complete chaos. She clung to her heritage and never developed a sense of independence in Hong Kong.

The juxtaposition of cultures created tension in the Woo marriage. Hung U Lan never learned English. Peter Woo, at 5'10", a foot taller than his wife, was fully Westernized. He made his living in the shipping business, which accorded him opportunities to travel. He played bridge, was a member of the Masonic Lodge, and was an avid dancer in a social set that did not include his wife. He became an inveterate gambler. In spite of difficulties, the marriage endured. Although there was no thought of divorce, there were discussions concerning the possibility of

Peter Woo taking a second wife. According to his daughter, that is the Chinese way.

The Woo union produced six children, four of whom were daughters. All were bestowed with Irish names by Peter Woo, including the youngest daughter, Carolyn, born in 1954. Carolyn's two brothers, a doctor and a lawyer, followed their father's lead and embraced the professional expectations of their father. The girls were raised without similar expectations. Woo's three sisters followed their mother's path, believing that education for Chinese women was not a high priority. None of them attended college. But Woo surprised them all. Even as a teenager, she defied their limited vision for girls and worked hard to shed the constraints of Chinese society and obtain a college education. This was a major rebellion in the Woo household.

Woo was greatly influenced by her nanny, Gaga, who joined the family eight years before Woo was born. Gaga was an uneducated servant girl who learned to read by standing outside the schoolroom of children she looked after. Gaga was a Buddhist who every morning would light incense, face the window, and kneel and bow until her head touched the floor while thanking the heavens and the earth. Gaga took care of Woo and instilled in her a discipline for hard work, respect for elders, honesty, and compassion for those who could not fend for themselves. These lessons are integral to Woo's personal philosophy and form the basis of her advice to younger generations.

One morning while stuffing envelopes as a favor to a sister, who was a secretary at Trans World Airlines, the teenaged Woo met a professor who was on sabbatical in Hong Kong. The professor advised her to seek an education at "his" school, Purdue University. The fortuitous meeting changed Woo's destiny. In a desperate effort to obtain admission to Purdue, Woo mastered the vocabulary necessary to achieve a credible score on the SAT examination by memorizing an abridged version of Webster's dictionary. She won acceptance in 1971 and left home the following year.

Woo arrived in America as an eager but frightened young woman at age 18 with her dictionary and few other worldly possessions; she had barely enough money to last one year. She stood on the precipice of a new life clutching the X-rays proving she did not have tuberculosis. She was under considerable pressure. There was no turning back. She could not even afford a ticket home. Gaga and her older siblings had provided money for this endeavor. She could not let them down. She could not fail.

"I worked as though the devil was chasing me," Woo says, describing her frenetic quest for a college education. Woo averaged 21 credit hours each semester during her first year at Purdue University in a headlong rush to obtain a bachelor's degree in economics in three years. She earned scholarships to pay for classes, but her budget was always strained. Woo could not afford to eat out, and she obtained free haircuts from students at the local beauty academy. She earned spending money by teaching religion classes to children and by tutoring Purdue football players in math. Despite her heavy class load, she graduated with honors and highest distinction. She remained in Lafayette for graduate work and just four years later earned a master's degree and her doctorate. "It's not the way I would advise young people to do it today," adds Woo, who is known as Dean Woo, the Martin J. Gillen Dean of the Mendoza College of Business and the Ray and Milann Siegfried Chair in Entrepreneurial Studies at the University of Notre Dame.

Where did Carolyn Y. Woo find the inner strength to succeed in spite of adversity and uncertainty in her young life? She is blessed with intellect, creativity, toughness, and resolve, all of which she has put to good use. She also has drawn strength from her culture. The "Y." of Woo's name stands for two things: Yau and Yan. Yan, a character she shares with her sisters, represents the Confucian teaching about the proper way people should relate to one another. Yau is more personal. Derived from her mother's name, it means delicate and refined—an accurate description of Woo, who is just a few inches taller than her mother.

As she started her new life in Indiana, Woo found a renewed faith and a new family in the Catholic Center at Purdue University. Although not

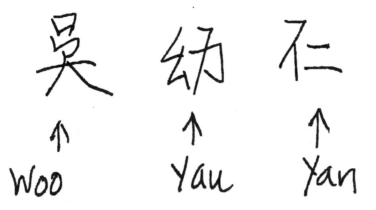

a churchgoer himself, Peter Woo insisted that his children be baptized, go to Catholic schools, and attend Mass. The Catholic school Woo attended from grades 1 through 12 was taught by the Maryknoll nuns who were missionary sisters headquartered in New York. After the Communist regime ousted them from China, the nuns settled in Hong Kong and established schools there. Not only did Woo learn to speak English from the sisters, but she learned to express her own ideas clearly. More importantly, she learned to imagine. The Maryknoll nuns planted in her seeds of independence and high achievement, all within the context of faith in God. With this connection to her faith and with the help of many friends among her roommates and classmates during her college career, Woo planted her Hoosier roots.

Those seeds grew along with her education. As Woo worked toward her Ph.D., she focused on weighty matters: strategic management and quantitative methods. Her doctoral dissertation explored how businesses could achieve success despite low market penetration—a theory running counter to conventional wisdom, which held that a business needed to garner a dominant share in its industry in order to make money. Woo's work was impressive enough that portions of the dissertation were published in 1981 and 1982 in the prestigious Harvard Business Review, an extraordinary achievement and a testament to its quality.

Perhaps not surprisingly, her work championed the underdog. She took issue with the prevailing belief that dominant companies achieve economies of scale through sheer size, leading to low-cost production and an enhanced bargaining position with customers and suppliers. Those advantages enable dominant players to dictate the market and relegate smaller competitors to marginal profitability and poor prospects. The big dog eats first, in other words. Woo's dissertation set a course for businesses aspiring to achieve large profits despite a low market share—describing how a company like Mrs. Fields Cookies could prevail in a world dominated by corporate giants such as Nabisco, for example. The work was radical but logical, and it launched Woo in her field. She has continued to research and publish corollaries to this theory. Woo maintains that service and professional support are very important for small companies seeking to distinguish themselves from those firms dominating the market.

The day after submitting her doctorial dissertation in 1979, Woo married David Bartkus, a Caucasian from Delaware. She retained the name of Woo in honor of her father. She and her husband have two children: Ryan Peter, who graduated from Notre Dame in 2007 and who is attending medical school at the University of Virginia, and Justin Edward, who is studying theology at Notre Dame. Although both children are native-born Hoosiers, they also have Chinese names and enjoy some Chinese customs, including two that are especially noteworthy. On the anniversaries of the birth and of the death of a deceased relative, family members gather in an effort to perpetuate their ancestor's memory, lighting candles around the photographs of the loved one and bowing three times together as a family. The family celebrates Chinese New Year by giving unmarried relatives small red packets with money inside. Woo looks forward to rare reunion opportunities with her far-flung siblings, a truly international affair. Her brothers- and sisters-in-law hail from China, the United States, Canada, Great Britain, the Philippines, and South Africa.

Woo has spent her entire academic career in Indiana, joining the Purdue faculty as an assistant professor in 1981 after a short stint as a planning analyst for General Motors. She rose to the post of associate executive vice president for academic affairs with significant responsibility for managing the university's academic programs. Woo was successful and happy at Purdue helping its business school and more particularly the MBA program achieve considerably improved rankings. Although she didn't know it, her growing reputation had caught the attention of another great university.

In 1996, Provost Nathan Hatch was given the task of finding and hiring the best candidate to lead the university's Mendoza College of Business. He found Woo, whose credentials were without peer. "No one else was seriously considered," Hatch said, and after a vigorous pursuit, Woo accepted the dean's position. The mission of the Mendoza College of Business is to foster academic excellence, professional effectiveness, and personal accountability, all while remaining faithful to Catholic teachings and values, a seemingly perfect fit for Woo. Perhaps as a result, the college has thrived under her leadership. Early in her administration, just after the completion of a beautiful new business school building, Woo demonstrated her commitment to providing faculty whatever they needed in order to achieve at the highest level. She went to the provost for help, telling him the university needed to do a better job of supporting faculty. "It's like athletes who don't have shoes but arrive at meets in a Cadillac," she told him. "We need to get shoes immediately." Hatch responded by devoting more of the university's financial resources to faculty salaries and support.

Within a decade of her arrival, the Mendoza College of Business consistently ranked high among all U.S. business schools. Publications, including *Business Week* and *U.S. News and World Report*, regularly include it in listings of the elite schools, a marked improvement over the pre-Woo years. While striving for excellence, the school has strengthened its roots with the Catholic Church, thereby accomplishing both major elements of the school's mission. Mendoza graduates are educated to care about every aspect of life, not just the profit-and-loss statement. Woo's professional goal as dean is to position the institution so that when the curriculum, research, and level of student engagement are judged, they will be deemed the gold standard of ethical leadership. Woo's colleagues have little doubt that goal will be achieved.

Woo's management style is a seamless meld of East and West. As a child in Hong Kong, she was raised to be mindful of hierarchy. According to Woo, proudly referring to her Asian roots, "The Eastern style is beneficial in that it helps you cultivate a sense of group interest. It says, 'I'm not in this for myself.'" The Chinese way is to manage in a manner that does not embarrass, but rather gives room to maneuver. Manners are an important part of Eastern protocol. It is important to preserve social dynamics so that there is rarely a situation when relationships completely break down. The Western style, on the other hand, is more competitive. Woo's U.S. education taught her to be more assertive, to articulate her thinking, and to understand the impact of that thought. The hybrid Woo style is one of energy, honesty, collegiality, and teamwork. Although aggressive, highly organized, and crisp in demeanor, she evinces sensitivity and great affection for her team and they love her in return.

In addition to her academic responsibilities, Woo serves on the board of directors for three Fortune 500 companies: Circuit City Stores, Inc., the third largest consumer electronics retailer in the United States; AON Corp., a leading provider of risk management and related services; and NiSource Inc., a company engaged in generation, transmission, storage, and distribution of natural resources. To Woo, board rooms are exciting places, often elegantly appointed and equipped with the latest in technology. Even more importantly, they are places where a diverse group of directors—recruited for their intelligence, knowledge, and good judgment—work diligently toward a common goal. Woo's fluency in the Chinese language and culture, combined with her expertise in Western business practices, is invaluable to companies seeking to transact global commerce. As China continues to realize its potential to be the world's largest producer, consumer, and major player on the economic scene, the demand for Woo and her skill set likely will become even greater. Woo is grateful for the opportunity to work with Circuit City, AON, and NiSource. As an academic it is important for her to continue to update her business knowledge in real time. As she puts it, "I'm in the rink versus being a spectator."

Woo also enjoys her service on not-for-profit boards, both local and national. In 2003, she became the first woman in eighty-seven years to chair the Association for the Advancement of Collegiate Schools of Business International, an alliance of organizations devoted to promoting and improving business administration and management programs. The organization accredits more than five hundred business schools in twenty-eight countries. Under Woo's leadership, AACSB International implemented new standards for accreditation, restructured the leadership committee, and helped schools develop the capabilities the new standards demanded. Woo also led the launch of the "Peace Through Commerce" initiative that advances the premise that business can be much more than a pathway to prosperity—it can be a catalyst for world peace. Under that program, business schools in partnership with commercial enterprises strive to bring seemingly disparate factions together.

Woo is also on the Board of Regents at the University of Portland, an affiliate of the Congregation of Holy Cross's Indiana Province, which founded the University of Notre Dame. The university is devoted to an education of the heart and mind by focusing on three central elements: teaching, faith, and service. The university has grown to a vibrant intellectual community of more than 3,200 students and 280 professors and is ranked among the top five schools in the West by *U.S. News and World Report*. It boasts some of the finest teachers in the country, and prides itself on providing a traditional, values-centered education attuned to the needs of every student. University president Reverend E. William Beauchamp is a former executive vice president of Notre Dame who worked with Woo on a number of matters. Upon his arrival in Oregon, he wasted no time in recruiting her to his board.

In a historic move, Catholic Relief Service in 2004 appointed Carolyn Woo as one of five lay individuals to serve on its board of directors—the first time in the agency's history that lay members have served in this capacity. Founded in 1943 by Catholic bishops in the United States, CRS works to assist the poor and disadvantaged outside the country alleviating human suffering, promoting development of all people, and fostering charity and justice throughout the world. CRS operates on five continents and in ninety-eight countries. Not long after joining the board, she and other CRS board members were dispatched to Banda Aceh, Indonesia, on the island of Sumatra to evaluate damage and help relief workers following a tsunami that devastated the region on the day after Christmas in 2004. Travel to areas of the world that are torn apart by disaster, war, extreme poverty, or AIDS gives Woo an opportunity to practice one of the important tenets of her faith—service to her fellow man.

Woo's professional accomplishments have led to another honor: an invitation to become a member of the elite Committee of One Hundred, comprised of prominent Chinese Americans who have achieved leadership positions in a broad range of professions, including business, art, and science. The committee was founded by a group of Chinese Americans, including architect I. M. Pei and musician Yo-Yo Ma. Its agenda is to promote the role of Chinese Americans in American society and to create relationships which foster understanding between China and the United States.

In addition to her many other talents, Woo plays the piano. Her mother insisted that she take piano lessons at age 4, though she needed a stool to climb up onto the piano bench. As a child, Woo was not pleased with this intrusion on her free play time, so she exhibited the independence that was to manifest itself later by unilaterally canceling her lessons without the knowledge or consent of her mother. Today she is proud of her skills as an amateur musician and although Woo does not have much time to play, she loves her piano. Given her drive, it is little surprise she has mastered many of the Chopin waltzes. Woo also enjoys flower arranging and gift wrapping, self-taught hobbies that give her an opportunity to relax. "Flower arranging is a form of expressing creativity and there is magic and energy when you do things with your hands," she says.

Above all, Woo is a mother, wife, and friend, who stands by those she loves in all situations. She has mastered the difficult task of balancing a professional and private life with an elegant philosophy: "People come first and God is in our every moment," she says.

She doesn't just believe the advice she offers young people—she lives it: "Be serious about the responsibilities you accept, whether it is in a student organization or a part-time job. Whenever you accept responsibility, take it seriously, do your very best, and don't let people down. Let people know that your presence can be counted upon. There is beauty, poetry, and grace when we execute to our very best. Although it is hard, try to do the right thing despite fear—fear of rejection or fear of not being good enough or fear of not belonging. Stare your insecurity in the face and do not give in."

According to the Woo philosophy everyone has a responsibility to try to make life work. "Focus on what you like and what you are good at. Focus on happiness," she advises. Woo found her happiness in the country of her choice. In 1996, she traveled with her proud family to South Bend, Indiana, to confirm that choice. In the presence of the Daughters of the American Revolution, she officially took an oath and became a citizen of the United States.

The devil is no longer chasing Carolyn Y. Woo, but she is still dreaming. She loves Notre Dame and has declined opportunities to be named president of another university. Although qualified in all other respects, Woo is ineligible to be considered for Notre Dame's presidency because she is not a priest of the Congregation of Holy Cross. Undeterred, Woo believes the work of God is not in titles. "He will put us where we can do the most good," she says.

At lunch with the U.S. and Chinese presidents, Woo remembered what it was like to be an immigrant. "I was awash with the sense of the many people who had made it possible for me to be at the White House—my teachers, my family, my brothers and sisters, my mentors. I felt they were all with me there. Am I dreaming?" One can only guess where her dreams will take this woman of achievement; this woman of faith.

Angela M. Brown

Lifetime of Preparation— Overnight Sensation

Since it was established in 1883, New York's Metropolitan Opera has been known as a venue for the great voices of the world. Extraordinary performances have come to be expected. So it was on Friday, October 29, 2004, when a nervous soprano was about to debut before a full house in Verdi's classic opera *Aida*. By 8:00 that evening, the orchestra had completed its tuning. The lights dimmed. The chandeliers slowly rose into the reaches of the ceiling, and the elegant gold silk curtain began to pull back and sweep up. The audience was ready.

The first aria, "Ritorna vincitor," went smoothly and was met with warm applause. Then the soprano relaxed and hit her stride. Her magnificent and nuanced performance captured the emotional range of the Ethiopian princess, Aida, from her brief happiness to her tragic decision to be buried alive with the Egyptian general she loved. It takes a special gift to master the role of Aida, and the audience knew it had witnessed something rare. The opera ended amid cries of "Brava!" and an immediate and extended standing ovation. Adoring fans rushed down the aisles proffering bouquets and throwing flowers onto the stage. After more than twenty years of hard work, Indianapolis native Angela Brown had become an overnight sensation. She cried as she thanked the audience profusely. The *New York Times* summed up her performance in four words: "At last, an Aida."

photo: Roni Ely

★ ★ ★

The middle of three children, Brown was born on December 1, 1963, to Freddie Mae and Walter C. Brown of Indianapolis, Indiana. Walter was a factory worker at Chrysler for forty-one years who rarely took a day off for sickness. At the time of his retirement, he was credited with six years of sick time. Walter was steady and careful. All of his advice to young Angela reflected that temperament.

Freddie Mae was a free spirit who operated a beauty shop in the basement of the family's home at Broadway and 30th streets before working for Methodist Hospital as a licensed practical nurse. Her interests were eclectic. She was always sketching. She took her artistic talent seriously and became a teacher at the Indianapolis Art League. Shoppers would pause at her kiosk at the Glendale Mall in front of the local retailer L.S. Ayres for many years while she created portraits from photographs. She was a singer in high school but curtailed a career, declining a scholarship offer from the Jordan School of Music at Butler University, in order to marry and have children. Perhaps it is out of regret for that decision that Freddie Mae enthusiastically encouraged her only daughter's musical career, which began at the age of 5 at the Mount Calvary Missionary Baptist Church where her grandfather Reverend Fred Harvey Moore presided.

Angela Brown attended Crispus Attucks High School, a predominantly black school in central Indianapolis. Named for a black man who was the first American to die in the Revolutionary War, the school is most famous for its Oscar Robinson–led state championship basketball team of 1955. But more importantly, Crispus Attucks earned national recognition for educational excellence and produced a number of business leaders and professionals in many fields, including the performing arts. At Crispus Attucks, Brown learned from teachers and role models such as Robert Fleck, her music teacher, whose encouragement made a lasting impression.

In her early teens, the reach and range of Brown's voice were evident, but the talent was raw. She sang mezzo soprano, which is a bit lower than a soprano—no lofty notes. During this time, Brown performed in high school theater and sang in gospel choirs citywide. She was one of the stars of the Crispus Attucks's musical programs, where she appeared in *Jesus Christ Superstar*, *Two Gentlemen of Verona*, and *Guys and Dolls*.

After graduating from Crispus Attucks in 1982, Brown attended Indiana University–Purdue University Indianapolis (IUPUI) and Ivy Tech, working toward a secretarial science degree while continuing to perform wherever she could, including regular roles in Indianapolis Civic Theatre productions. She sang gospel and rhythm and blues, and even performed in a jazz band. Brown was a member of the Greater Indianapolis Youth for Christ Choir and the Steve Coleman Concert Choir, for which she was one of the lead soloists. One summer, she also performed at C.B. Kendall Musicale, a cabaret restaurant in Indianapolis. Ironically, that summer, in her first operatic performance, she was an Ethiopian slave in the chorus of the Indianapolis Opera's *Aida*. It was during this time that Brown realized she could become a professional entertainer. Another Civic Theatre performer, Mary Bentley, had secured a part in the Broadway hit *Dream Girls* and recommended Brown to her producers for an understudy role. Bentley's parents drove Brown to New York for a private audition with Michael Bennett, the director and conceiver of *Dream Girls*. She did not land the part because she was only 19 years old. Bennett felt she was too young—too green. But the episode started Brown thinking, "Maybe I can do this for a living."

Brown's interest in opera was kindled by chance. One day, she watched a woman sing a jingle on television. Dressed in a beautiful gown, she was touting the United Negro College Fund. Brown thought to herself, "Oh, my goodness. This is a black woman and listen to how she's singing." It was beloved Metropolitan Opera soprano Leontyne Price. Although Brown ached to perform, she also wanted to please her father, who insisted, "You can sing, Angie, just have something to fall back on." Her mother, on the other hand, counseled her to concentrate on her stage career.

In 1984, Brown's younger brother, Aaron, contracted bacterial meningitis while at boot camp for the National Guard and died suddenly. The death of her brother and that of her grandfather about six months later sent Brown into a deep spiritual search that led her to become a Seventh Day Adventist. Her quest was to become a singing evangelist. She was advised to attend Oakwood College—now Oakwood University—in Huntsville, Alabama, because its mission was to prepare students to serve God and humanity, and because the college had produced great singers and preachers. Brown, by then a little older than the average freshman, attended Oakwood for five years, receiving bachelor's degrees in music and arts in 1991.

Brown's talent was wondrous and diverse, but it needed to be channeled in order for her to command a place on the world's stage. One day one of her peers at Oakwood counseled her, "Angela, you know you sing gospel music very well. You can stand with the best of them, toe-to-toe. You can go out of here and have a big gospel singing career. You can have recordings. You can do all that, but when you sing classical music, you are head and shoulders above everyone else." Brown decided to test her friend's theory, and in her last year and a half at Oakwood, she concentrated solely on opera. She loved it.

By then determined to make opera her career, Brown knew she needed more formal training. She auditioned at Indiana University, home to one of the world's most outstanding and acclaimed music schools. The IU Jacobs School of Music plays a key role in educating performers, scholars, and music educators who influence music performance and education around the globe. Brown's audition went well. At IU she was introduced to her future teacher, Virginia Zeani, by her teacher at Oakwood, Ginger Beazley.

In 1991, Brown enrolled in a master's program in vocal performance at IU and immersed herself in classical music under the tutelage of the renowned Zeani. Zeani, who had reigned as "prima donna assoluta" at the Teatro dell'Opera in Rome for twenty-five years, said to her new pupil, "The blood of Verdi courses through your veins." In addition to studying opera, Brown took classes in French, German, and Italian, the languages of classical music. On campus she landed the role of Fata Morgana in *The Love for Three Oranges* and the title role in *Ariadne auf Naxos*. She was also the soprano soloist in the Verdi Requiem, a musical setting of the Catholic funeral mass. She told her graduate course counselor, "I see myself being the next Leontyne Price. I want to sing in all the opera houses of the world."

Brown financed her education at IU by working at the university's African American Arts Institute in Bloomington, where she was the vocal coach for the IU Soul Revue. In exchange, the university paid her a stipend and covered a portion of her tuition. She supplemented her income with student loans and professional fees earned by singing for the university, usually with acclaimed pianist Charles Webb, the dean of the School of Music. In 1995, Brown met Webb's daughter-in-law, Janet Jarriel, a graduate student studying arts administration at IU's School of Music. The women became good friends and often discussed their goals and aspirations. One day Brown said, "Why don't we try to do this together and see how it goes?" Jarriel became Brown's agent, a relationship that has endured.

During her years at IU, Brown participated in a competition called the Metropolitan Opera National Council Auditions. Three times, she advanced to the regionals by winning the district contest, but did not make it to the finals in New York City. In 1997, at age 33—the last year she could compete—Brown won the district contest once more and went to the regionals in Cincinnati. She won. Part of winning was a two-week, all-expenses-paid trip to New York City, where she joined twenty-two other regional contest winners. The group was invited to attend an opera every night and took master classes from some of the great opera coaches. The finalists performed on the Metropolitan Opera stage and used dressing rooms that had been occupied by legends such as Luciano Pavarotti. It was a heady time for a young woman. The ongoing competition reduced the field to ten national winners. Brown survived.

Winning the National Council Auditions enhanced Brown's reputation and enabled her to land numerous appearances, but winning a competition can take one only so far. Brown needed to return to the Met to formally audition for the main stage. She left IU in 1997, just a few credits short of her degree. Her voice was maturing and her career was calling. For almost three years, Brown performed around the country, commuting from Indianapolis to New York City for auditions. In the fall of 1999, she decided that in order to pursue her career seriously, she had to move there.

Brown found a boardinghouse in Queens, one of the five boroughs of NYC, that charged $80 a week. The money she had saved was enough to live on for six weeks with little to spare. She arrived in the rain. Her luggage had broken and her clothes were soaking wet. Once inside the boardinghouse, she spied a bug crawling across the wall. A cat ran by, rubbing against her leg. (Brown is allergic to cats.) Tired, she unpacked as best she could and went to sleep. When she awoke the next day, she was covered from head to toe with flea bites.

Later that week on the way to a recital, she met fellow opera singer Jeryl Cunningham, who also had graduated from Oakwood. They agreed to become roommates in the Bronx—a little closer, a little cleaner, and a little less costly. The first six months, she slept on a broken trundle bed, often without heat. Brown lived in that Bronx apartment for five years. She continued to make progress with her singing career in other opera houses, in recitals, and with orchestras. She learned, however, "that living in New York City takes all the money you've got."

Brown auditioned at the Met through a program that allows past National Council Audition winners to apply for grants. Her voice had gained richness and maturity since 1997, something that was evident to the staff at the Met. She was called back to audition on the main stage. Brown has the big voice required for Verdi operas. She can be heard over the orchestra and she can fill the hall. She also has pianissimos, high floaty notes so soft that Brown can give them "ebb and flow like the Nile."

During the second audition, Brown asked for a glass of water. Someone in the first row answered, "Honey, if you keep singing like that you can have anything you want." When that second audition ended, the secretary to the general manager was in tears. She said, "Angela you are beautiful. I have a feeling about these things. I've been here for years. You're going to be singing here one day, I just know it. I just feel it." The next day she received another call from the Met offering her an under-study role—called a "cover" in the opera world—for *Aida* during the 2000–2001 season. Covers make less than half the salary of lead singers and must be ready to step in at any moment. Unfortunately, she did not have an opportunity to sing a lead role in any of the six performances of *Aida* that season. She was awarded additional covers in 2002. Would she always be a cover?

One afternoon in late 2002, while another soprano was rehearsing for her debut as Aida, Brown got her big chance. The soprano would debut in two days, but first she had to make it through the sitzprobe, a final rehearsal with the whole orchestra, including the conductor and the cast but without acting, scenery, or costumes. She whispered to Brown, "I don't want to blow my wad in the sitzprobe and not be able to sing my debut, so be ready tomorrow, just in case."

The next day, the soprano approached Brown and reminded her that she might be needed. Brown dutifully warmed up, and the soprano said, "I'll tell you what. I'm going to sing the first line and if I feel like I should not continue, I'll let you know." She sang the first line, then sat down and gave Brown a wink. Brown's knees were shaking; she had never worked with that conductor and she had not sung an aria with the Metropolitan Opera orchestra since 1997. But she sang. And she sang. The rehearsal lasted from 11 AM until 2 PM. Following an hour break, the covers did another total run-through. She sang *Aida* twice that day. "I was pooped," Brown recalls. She was so tired that on the train back to the Bronx she forgot to turn her cell phone back on. When she arrived home she retrieved her messages. Janet Jarriel was frantic. She said, "Angela, Angela, what did you do? The Met called and offered you two performances and twelve covers for the 2004 season." The 2003 season had already been cast.

Brown's sensational debut was witnessed by family and friends—many of whom had seen her in an Indianapolis Opera production of *Aida* in 2001. Remembering that performance, busloads and planeloads of her fans trekked to the Met. Oakwood College and Indiana University were represented that evening as well. The reaction was exuberant. Critics described Brown's performance and her voice as one would a fine wine. A week later in a front-page story in the *New York Times*, critic Ann Midgette thrilled Brown with the following comparison: "Ms. Brown is in the tradition of Leontyne Price, another church-bred singer with a big, warm voice capable of trumpeting high notes or floating beautiful, melting soft ones."

In 2005, both of Brown's parents became ill. In order to be near them and assist with their care, she returned to Indianapolis to live. She has commuted to New York City and other venues ever since. Brown loves the slower rhythms of Indianapolis—preferring that pace to the hustle and bustle and tension of the big city. She is an Indianapolis Colts and Indiana Pacers fan. Although her father passed away from mesothelioma, she continues to support her mother. One day she would like a family of her own.

Brown reprised her role in *Aida* at the Met in 2007. The performance was reviewed by Joshua Rosenblum of the *Opera News*: "Angela Brown, who sang her first *Aida* at the Met in 2004, seems to have it all—a creamy, spacious lirico-spinto voice, unerring musical phrasing, solid non-stagy acting and immaculately floating high notes capable of conveying the full depth of her character's suffering. She also has an endearing, toothy grin that lights up the stage during Aida's brief moments of happiness."

Brown continues to star at the Met, not only in *Aida* but in other operas as well. Following her triumphant appearance there, she debuted at the National Opera of Paris in 2007 as Amelia in Verdi's *Un Ballo in Maschera*, which she reprised at the Met in 2008. *Un Ballo* has more agility than *Aida*, moving faster and requiring a lower range. "It's a fun sing," Brown says. She has sung at the preeminent opera houses throughout the world, making her a true international star.

Despite Brown's crowded performance calendar, she finds time for many related activities. She has recorded a number of CDs, including one featuring her favorite Verdi arias and another titled *Mosaic* with her favorite spirituals. She drew from her early experiences in church for the African American spiritual concept of this CD, performing with guitarist Tyron Cooper and pianist Joseph Joubert. *Mosaic* was produced by Everett McCorvey of the American Spiritual Ensemble in Lexington, Kentucky—a group founded in 1995 to keep the American Negro spiritual alive. According to Brown, the original spirituals were written for the classical stage to be sung by classical singers. In a review of *Mosaic*, David Hurwitz of *Classics Today* wrote, "The principal emotion here is joy. [Brown's] voice is gorgeous: pure, rich and strong." Brown also recorded a television program with the Indianapolis Chamber Orchestra, *Homecoming with Angela Brown*, which aired on public television in Indianapolis and throughout the country.

For opera companies that want to enlighten, broaden, and add to the diversity of their audiences, Brown fashioned a clever one-person show, *Opera from a Sistah's Point of View*. Its goal is to bring opera to audiences that normally would not attend. Brown has performed this concert not only in African American churches but also at corporate functions. The program mixes popular arias with witty conversation. For example, when discussing *Aida*, she tells her audience that "no man is worth climbing into that tomb. There are other men out there. There are other fish in the sea. Honey, you can find another man, it's not that good. Ladies, is it ever that good?" People relax and laugh. They understand that opera is really not that difficult and that one does not have to miss out on this wonderful expression of art just because it seems daunting at first.

For those who wish to pursue a singing career, she advises, "Enjoy your work—keep singing, pay attention to good advice, and seek help. Turn away from the people who discourage you and keep positive people in your path." Brown worries that the example she has set may be intimidating to others. She continues, "Don't let anyone define success for you. You have to define it for yourself. You can be inspired by me. But I would say, go beyond me. You shouldn't count anything as a failure if you have the thought to do it and you start to move toward it. If you don't necessarily get to the pinnacle that first time you try, you've got to keep on pressing through. You have to keep trying and any success, count it as success." Drawing from her childhood in church and her experience at Oakwood, she says, "Place your life in the master's hand and the master is the Lord for me. I believe you have to have something higher than you that you look to for aid and for help and then after that the sky is the limit."

Brown believes that when the Lord gives you that extra measure, you're responsible for helping someone else along the way. Brown enjoys giving back. She performs free concerts to support charities. She takes pleasure in supporting the United Negro College Fund. Leontyne Price would be proud.

In 2006, Brown was presented the IU African American Arts Institute's Herman C. Hudson Alumni Award, which recognizes outstanding contributions made in the arts. She was the first recipient of the award. Brown credited people who believed in her such as Robert Fleck, Virginia Zeani, and Eleanor Starks, the choir director who gave young Angela her first solo at her grandfather's church. She also remembered with fondness her first music teacher, Miss Rose at School 76.

With a voice that reaches the heights and with roots that are set deep in Hoosier soil, Angela Brown has never lost sight of her goal and has never given up. She is a diva with a heart as big and as soft as her magnificent voice.

Ora Hirsch Pescovitz

The Juggler

r. Ora Hirsch Pescovitz has not one but three demanding jobs. She's president and chief executive officer of Indianapolis's Riley Hospital for Children, one of the top children's hospitals in the nation. Plus, she's executive associate dean for research at the Indiana University School of Medicine, as well as IU's interim vice president for research affairs. So it might seem surprising how the 51-year-old spends her "free" time: leading self-help workshops. In a typical session on a chilly fall evening in 2007, she talked with two dozen doctors about how to achieve their personal and professional goals, while striking a balance between the two.

"If you are going to 'kill your lions' and achieve your life goals," Pescovitz told the group, "first make sure you're focusing on what's truly important."

It's an apt topic, because few have done it as well as she has. Through intricate planning and prioritizing—and a nearly manic energy level—Pescovitz has risen to become one of the nation's top hospital administrators and one of its foremost pediatric endocrinologists. Endocrinologists treat disorders related to hormones and glands. At Riley, that often means working with children recovering from cancer who are wrestling with complications of chemotherapy.

It's a career Pescovitz loves, but not at the expense of family. She and her husband, Mark, a transplant surgeon who serves as vice chairman of

research in IU School of Medicine's Department of Surgery, wed nearly three decades ago and continue to have a strong marriage. Together, they have raised three children: Aliza is a law student at American University in Washington, D.C. Ari graduated from IU in 2008 with three degrees—in biology, anthropology, and fine arts—with plans to pursue a graduate degree in architecture from the University of Cincinnati. The youngest, Naomi, is a journalism student at the Medill School of Journalism at Northwestern University in Evanston, Illinois.

It wasn't always easy.

"I did go through a period when I struggled a little bit to become the mother my mother was, and the professional my mother wanted me to be. My mother was a fantastic mother, but she didn't work outside the home," Pescovitz says.

Bella Hirsch, Pescovitz's mother, set high expectations for her daughter and three sons while simultaneously imbuing them with the belief they could achieve anything. It was a disciplined upbringing. Television was limited, and each child was expected to play a musical instrument and practice several hours a day. Bella kept an immaculate home and made every meal from scratch; as a child, Pescovitz never ate a TV dinner.

When she became a mother herself in 1984, Pescovitz realized she was going to have to make choices.

"I went through a very rigorous process of deciding what things I needed to do with my children to ensure that I would be the best mother possible, and what I could give up that my mother did for me, or with me, that I wasn't going to do," she says.

She also hunted for shortcuts. One important discovery: frozen onions. "What an amazing thing!" she says. "I didn't like chopping onions, and it takes a long time, and it makes me cry. I realized I could still make pretty good–tasting things with someone else chopping the onions, and my children would never know."

Pescovitz believes in the concept of a "mentor quilt" rather than a life patterned after any one person's. She has had dozens of mentors and role models, including many of her colleagues at Riley and the IU School of

Medicine. A key mentor early in Pescovitz's career was Dr. D. Lynn Loriaux, a scientist at the National Institutes of Health in Bethesda, Maryland, where Pescovitz had a fellowship in the early 1980s.

"Dr. Loriaux's motto was always 'Go for it!' Whether I had a good research idea or a bad one, he always encouraged me to pursue it with vigor," Pescovitz recalls.

The examples both her parents set also left a lasting impression.

Richard G. Hirsch is honorary life president of the World Union for Progressive Judaism, the international body of Reform Judaism, which is the largest Jewish religious movement in the world. In the 1960s, he was a prominent rabbi active in the civil rights movement and marched with Martin Luther King Jr. in Selma, Alabama, and Washington, D.C. He also founded and led the Religious Action Center in Washington, D.C., which provided office space to King during his frequent visits to the capital. King's eldest son, Martin Luther King III, once called Rabbi Hirsch "a living symbol of the Jewish passion for social justice and the special bond between the black and Jewish communities."

Bella Rozencweig grew up in brutal conditions in Russia during World War II. Raised by a single mother, she sometimes starved, which stunted her growth (she grew to be just 4'11"). As a teenager after the war, Bella spent two years working as a nurse at a displaced person's camp in Germany. Later, she made her way to Israel. She was on the first boat to land there after Israel became a state in 1948, and for several years she worked as a nurse in the Israeli army.

In 1954, Bella traveled to Denver to visit relatives who had survived the Holocaust. While there, she landed a job as a nurse at a summer camp where Richard Hirsch was director. They fell in love and married that fall. Richard and Bella raised their family in a middle-class neighborhood in Bethesda, Maryland. They led a life of privilege compared with what Bella had experienced, and she wanted her children to make the most of it.

The Hirsches ingrained in their children the Judaic principle of Tikkun olam—a Hebrew phrase meaning "repairing the world" or "perfecting the world." They were expected to pursue service careers in which they could make a difference in the world and make it a better place. Two of her bothers are doctors; Raphael is chief of pediatric rheumatology at the Children's Hospital of Pittsburgh and Emmet is director of obstetrics at Evanston Northwestern Hospital in Illinois; the third, Ammiel, is a lawyer who became a rabbi and is now chief rabbi at the Stephen Wise Free Synagogue in Manhattan.

While respecting their father's achievements, Ora and her siblings also were part of an underground club called RKs (Rabbi's Kids). "We had lots of fun making fun of how seriously the clergy took themselves sometimes," she says. "We always knew their human foibles even though they seemed so righteous from the pulpit."

Pescovitz recalls that when she was 10 or 11, she told her mother she wanted to become a psychologist. Her mother suggested she become a psychiatrist instead, because then she'd have a medical degree and be able to write her own prescriptions. Besides, her mother said, she could become a psychiatrist with the same number of years of schooling. (Years later, when Pescovitz was in medical school, she finally realized that wasn't true.)

"It was my mother, in particular, who, through her own life example and by pushing me, really drove me to see that I could do a lot more than maybe other girls my age felt they could do," Pescovitz says.

By high school, she was weighing whether to become a doctor or pursue a career as a concert pianist. She was beginning to come to grips with the fact that she wasn't good enough to achieve her musical dreams when she signed up for a ninth-grade course called research and development that cemented her decision. Students had to design and execute a year-long experiment. She decided to evaluate whether plants would grow better if they were surrounded by no music, classical music, or music of the Beatles. The study didn't exactly revolutionize science. "What I learned at the end of the year was that I wasn't good at growing any plants," she says.

Even so, "I was thrilled by the idea that you could ask and answer questions by designing the proper experiment. You could learn something that would have applications," Pescovitz says. "Somehow, I think it was then that I decided I would like to one day become a physician-scientist."

Back then, around 1970, medicine was a career mostly for men. But Pescovitz didn't consider it to be beyond her grasp. She didn't mind being the only woman in research and development. In fact, as a girl going through puberty, she savored the extra attention.

"Part of the reason I don't think I ever felt intimidated by anything was my parents," Pescovitz says. "They always instilled in me the idea that there were no limits to what I could accomplish, short of my own imagination of what I might want to do, and my own drive and hard work."

After high school, Pescovitz enrolled at Northwestern University, where she'd been accepted into an elite program that squeezed college and medical school into six years, instead of the normal eight. (Pescovitz completed it in a little more than five.) On her first day there, she met Mark, who was a year ahead of her in the program. They weren't immediately a couple. She had dated lots of other men by the time they married five years later.

The couple shares core beliefs about religion, money, politics, and child-rearing. Yet in other ways, they're quite different. "People who are friends with us probably wonder how we are married. We are very vocal in disagreements. We disagree loudly," she says. "I actually like loud. It's something I seek. My husband doesn't. He is quiet."

In medical school, pediatrics was the last specialty Pescovitz had in mind. The thinking of the time was that female medical students should become pediatricians, since women are good with children. Pescovitz was determined to do the unexpected. She went so far as to delay her pediatric rotation until her senior year, after she was supposed to have made up her mind on a specialty.

But when she started doing the work, she found herself drawn to pediatrics. She thought many pediatricians viewed the world as she did and had similar values. She also liked helping patients whose medical conditions were no fault of their own. One frustration of working with adult patients, she says, is that many of their medical conditions might have been avoided had they lived a healthier lifestyle and avoided smoking or other dangerous behaviors.

She was drawn to the subspecialty of endocrinology by the intellectual challenge of solving daunting medical puzzles. "It's a specialty where there are very complex questions and problems that manifest themselves in different ways," she says. "The good news is once you have been through this challenging and exciting period of discovery of what is wrong, there are often good treatments."

Pescovitz moved to Minneapolis in 1979 to start her residency at the University of Minnesota, joining her husband, who already had begun his residency there. It was the first of four moves she made to follow Mark, who had narrower career options because of his transplantation specialty. Two years later, they moved to Washington, D.C., where he would spend four years at the National Institutes of Health doing research. Ora did a fellowship at NIH, working with other scientists researching the emerging field of precocious puberty, the onset of puberty in children as young as infancy. It's a condition that, if left untreated, can cause serious problems later in life.

Pescovitz left in 1985 for Minnesota, where her husband needed to finish his residency. It was a difficult move, she says, because she was fascinated by her NIH work and initially didn't find a job in Minnesota. In 1988, they moved again, this time to Indianapolis, where Mark had landed a position at the IU School of Medicine. IU soon brought her aboard as well, and just two years later she became director of pediatric endocrinology, an administrative post that allowed her to continue to do her own research. She continued her work on precocious puberty there, spearheading research that led to what now is the conventional therapy for the condition.

Pescovitz's other major research achievement was discovering a new hormone. "We don't know what it does," she says. Even so, "I'm proud of it. One of the things that is so exciting is that of course it was there, but no one else knew about it until I found it."

Through the years, Pescovitz has picked up additional responsibilities. As executive associate dean for research affairs since 2000, she is responsible for all the medical school's research programs, which bring in nearly $250 million a year in grants and contracts. She also oversees the eight-year-old Indiana Genomics Initiative. That effort—funded with $155 million from the Indianapolis-based Lilly Endowment—laid the groundwork for

BioCrossroads, the state's life science economic development initiative. It also has helped fund creation of new research labs and the hiring of top researchers, elevating the national stature of Indiana's biotechnology push.

Despite those new roles, Pescovitz continued to do her own research until 2004, when she became Riley's CEO. That was a career-defining promotion, because in accepting it she had no choice but to give up research, which she loves. At the time, "I always looked for the opportunity to have the greatest impact possible, and so I realized that it was possible to have more impact on more people through administration than might have been possible in my own individual work," she says. A year after taking the top job, Pescovitz helped roll out a $500 million, ten-year plan to elevate Riley into the top echelon of children's hospitals in the United States. She and Kevin O'Keefe, CEO of the Riley Children's Foundation, were instrumental in raising the money.

The plan already is yielding results. In 2007, *Child* magazine ranked Riley the eleventh-best children's hospital in the nation. Pescovitz wants it to make the top ten by 2010 and the top five by 2015. Construction began in 2006 on a ten-story, $470 million addition to Riley. Hospital officials hope the best facilities will attract more research dollars and top researchers and specialists, ultimately improving the care that children receive.

"Attracting leaders in pediatric medicine will not only enhance Riley's quality of care. It will also directly impact our state's efforts to grow the life sciences sector of the economy," Pescovitz said in announcing the plan.

Richard Schreiner, the IU pediatrics department chairman who hired Pescovitz, says she has excelled in every area of academic medicine, from patient care, teaching, and research to administration and advocacy on behalf of children.

When she came to the university, it had just one pediatric endocrinologist, along with one physician in a closely related specialty, says Schreiner, who now is Riley's physician-in-chief. It now has twelve, and is a national leader in the field.

What's most remarkable, he says, is that "she does all this with a most nurturing approach."

"I know a few other people in academic medicine in pediatrics who are just as productive and successful as Ora is," he adds. "But the difference between those few people and Ora is she leaves no human collateral along the road."

Indeed, Pescovitz doesn't talk or act like a no-holds-barred manager.

"I see my work, just like I see being a mother, as being primarily about creating an environment in which others will exceed me and do their best work and reach their potential," she says.

Pescovitz acknowledges academia isn't the easiest of fields for women. The demanding seven-year span when faculty are working toward and getting tenure coincides with women's peak reproductive years. She thinks universities should do a better job of accommodating women in light of that reality.

When she came to IU, all three of her children were under the age of 5. She was able to overcome the obstacles by working astonishingly hard. She typically gets up on weekdays by 5 AM (she sets her alarm for 5:20 AM as a backup) and is at work by 6:30.

These days, she often has a dinner meeting and will do additional work afterward. To maximize her productivity on the thirty-minute commute between Riley's main hospital downtown and her Carmel home, she drives a car with a hands-free phone.

"I don't know how she maintains the intensity of her work minute after minute, hour after hour, day after day, year after year," Schreiner says.

"I do work hard," Pescovitz acknowledges. But she doesn't believe her accomplishments are beyond the reach of other women. She wants to inspire others, not intimidate them.

"They say I don't sleep. It's not true, actually," she says, adding that she typically goes to bed by 11 PM.

Pescovitz says she makes time for non-work activities, such as exercising, reading books for pleasure, supporting arts and civic organizations, and spending time with her husband. One of their favorite activities is to curl up in bed and watch a movie.

As her schedule allows, she also serves as co-host of *Sound Medicine*, a weekly radio program on Indianapolis's WFYI 90.1 FM and other public radio stations around the state.

Time management and prioritizing are key, Pescovitz asserts. "Be sure to keep your eye on the ball in terms of what is important and recognize that perfection is the enemy of good," she says.

Pescovitz concluded that it was important for her and Mark to give the children their baths. But she hired someone else to do the laundry, since the children wouldn't care who washed the clothes, as long as they were clean. She also was committed to having family dinners most nights, but decided it wasn't necessary to cook everything from scratch, as her mother would have done.

When her children were in day care, she would halt work at 5:30 PM no matter what because the center closed at 6:00. But, as was the case throughout their childhood, she'd bring work home to do in the evening—something she'd do without any tinge of guilt.

"They had work to do, too," she says. "I think Mark and I set a wonderful example for them. There was a family expectation that after dinner, they would practice their instruments, or do their homework, or read a book, while we were doing the same."

She also learned a few tricks to avoid unproductive down time. When her daughter Naomi was captain of the North Central High School dance team—which performed at halftime at basketball games—Naomi's coach marveled that Pescovitz didn't allow her busy schedule to get in the way of attending all the games. In fact, she didn't actually see the games. She would breeze in right before halftime, then leave after the dance team's two-minute performance. It became such a routine that the woman at the entrance would waive her in without making her buy a ticket.

She has similar strategies to maximize her work time. These days, she has an office at Riley and another in a nearby IU building. She sometimes avoids walking between the two because she loves to gab. She knows she'll see friends or colleagues and become engrossed in a fifteen-minute conversation.

But Pescovitz hasn't always felt she had her life—and her priorities—figured out. At times, she second-guessed herself.

Years ago, she recalls, her son had forgotten something he needed for school, so she drove back into her neighborhood at a time of day she usually wasn't there. She enviously watched mothers with mugs of coffee in hand waiting for their children to be picked up by the school bus.

The sight set her mind whirring.

"I cried during the drive back downtown, because on that day I actually had this vision of what my life would have been like had I made another set of choices," she says. "I fantasized about what those women were going to do the rest of the day. I had visions of them finishing their coffee together. Then they were going to play tennis. Then I thought they'd have a manicure. Then maybe they were going to go out to lunch. Then maybe they were going to make cookies so they'd be ready by 3 o'clock when the children got off the bus."

Pescovitz says she recovered when she got to work and met with a cancer patient, a child whose quality of life was going to be better because of her care. While Pescovitz isn't critical of the decisions the women in her neighborhood made, she concluded she was doing more good by juggling career and family than if she were a stay-at-home mom.

One of the keys to making things work, she says, was hiring staff to help with the children and with housekeeping. She had live-in help until her children were teenagers. She calls hiring housekeepers "an essential component of being able to achieve this balance, especially since, like my mother, I demand a clean house."

Early on, she says, she spent more money on that help than she was earning. She was fine with that, because she wasn't working primarily for money, and knew she'd be earning more as her career progressed.

While other women might not have the financial means to make that choice, she thinks more would if they measured the value of their professional contributions in nonmonetary ways. "I think people tend not to realize how much value there can be in making a contribution beyond your family," she says.

Pescovitz's professional contributions already have been substantial. But she's only in her early 50s. So the prime of her career still lies ahead.

What's next? Pescovitz isn't sure. But in 2007, she was a finalist to become president of Indiana University. The board of trustees ultimately chose another veteran IU administrator, Michael McRobbie. She says she has no hard feelings and admires McRobbie. In fact, Pescovitz agreed to serve as McRobbie's vice president for research administration on an interim basis. In that role, she oversees research administration, as well as compliance with the complex rules governing it, for all eight IU campuses. It's a tremendous undertaking. The IU system received about $400 million in sponsored grants in its latest fiscal year.

Still, Pescovitz admits that not getting the university's biggest job was devastating. She says she had been lobbied by faculty in Bloomington and Indianapolis to seek the post, and spent six months deciding whether to become a candidate.

"I don't do anything half-heartedly," she says. "I went full force after the job, and I was looking forward to doing it."

Choosing between McRobbie and Pescovitz was a tough call for trustees. Days before McRobbie got the nod, IU trustee Philip Eskew said, "I think both of them are eminently qualified. We have two great leaders, either of which we'd be happy with."

Pescovitz says this wasn't the first time she's experienced a professional disappointment. When she decided to give up research, she was acknowledging she never would achieve her dream of winning a Nobel Prize.

She believes in setting the highest of goals, even if that means sometimes falling short. Her philosophy: "Shoot for the stars, and if you miss you'll land on the moon."

That mindset suggests Pescovitz eventually will leave Riley for a new challenge. As she tells participants in her self-help sessions, "Most successful people, while they are happy, they are not content."

So, perhaps after leaving her mark on Hoosier medicine and the health and well-being of many children, this multitalented juggler will find new ways to make Indiana a better place.

The good news is she now considers herself a Hoosier, through-and-through. "My husband and I love Indiana," she says. "We feel it has been good for us, and we love being here."

Mary Bolk

☆

A Woman of Valor
in an Army of Men

In 2006, on the outskirts of Mosul in the northern part of Iraq dubbed "Mortar City," members of the 399th Combat Support Hospital were relaxing in their metal 8x16 container housing units when the unmistakable sound of artillery shattered the air. Incoming! A mortar smashed through the roof of one trailer-like structure, hit a bed, and flew out the window into another unit, where it bounced around before landing intact fifteen feet from Mary Bolk. Although it inflicted extensive damage, it did not detonate. "I was a lucky girl," Bolk sighs.

Such attacks happen fast. Those who survive learn to scramble. Insurgents drive nearby in small Toyota pickup trucks, launch the mortars and take off. They usually come in threes—as the first mortar lands, the next one is already on its way. By the time the second one hit the roof of their hospital, Bolk and her team were safely in the bunkers. The third mortar tore the steel wall off the back of another building. Although Bolk was frightened, she was battle-tested. This was her second tour of duty in Iraq—just another day at the office for Bolk, an attractive blond who is just as comfortable in a straw hat as a combat helmet.

★ ★ ★

Mary Bolk was born December 18, 1955, in the Gibson County town of Princeton, in southwest Indiana. Before she could walk, the family—

including her two older sisters—moved twenty-five miles to Vincennes, a rural community of about twenty-six thousand people. While in middle school, Bolk again was uprooted for a move to Columbus, Indiana, where her father, William, had accepted a chemical engineering job with Crowder Engineering. Three years later, the family again followed her father's career, this time to Indianapolis, where Bolk has lived ever since. Bolk's mother, Patricia, didn't have much trouble finding jobs as they moved, since she was an elementary school teacher.

Bolk grew up a tomboy. In Vincennes she loved to ride with friends, not just horses but whatever was in the pen—whether it was cows, goats, or pigs. "We rode them because we didn't know any better; you learned to stay on," she says. Bolk was the only one in the family scratching poison ivy every summer from climbing trees, picking berries, and enjoying the outdoors in Vincennes's Gregory Park. One afternoon she and her friend Melanie Swonder borrowed guns from a neighbor's gun rack and shot the water moccasins and copperheads that had invaded their swimming hole. They didn't know children were not supposed to do that. She was indeed a lucky girl.

Bolk is the baby of the family, doted upon by her parents and sisters. She delights in reminding her family, "I didn't spoil me, you did." All three of the Bolk girls made a career of health care, although her sisters are now retired. Eldest child Threasa Angela (Tabbie) was a medical technologist with an MBA from Duke University. Middle sister Ellen Denise was a dental assistant. Bolk's interest in nursing was kindled by her godmother, Vivian Bouvey, a nurse from Vincennes and her mother's first cousin.

After graduating from high school in 1974, Bolk earned an associate's degree in nursing from Indiana University Kokomo. After two years working at the IU Medical Center's neurosurgical intensive care unit, Bolk returned to school—this time to Purdue University. Although hungry for more education, she wasn't even sure what she wanted to learn. Perhaps fascinated by her father's profession, she majored in engineering and technology, earning her first bachelor's degree in 1982. The degree, coupled with her nursing credentials, put her on a management track.

Upon graduation, she secured a position at Westview Hospital in Indianapolis running the surgery department, where she led an effort to build a new surgical wing. The achievement was significant but it wasn't enough to satisfy her desire to give back to the community.

In nursing school, Bolk had been enthralled with the story of Florence Nightingale, the original battlefield nurse and a pioneer in the Red Cross movement. Nightingale was known by British soldiers in the Crimean War as the "lady with the lamp" because of the late hours she worked tending to the sick and wounded. Even after Bolk had developed a successful career, she felt something was missing. "I got the bug that I wasn't really doing enough for people. I had no responsibilities so I could follow in Florence Nightingale's footsteps," Bolk explains. "I called the Army Reserve recruiter and said, 'I'm an operating room nurse. I want to sign up. What am I getting myself into?'" She joined as a second lieutenant in 1985.

The Middle East has always been a bad neighborhood, and Iraq often has been the bully. After Iraq invaded neighboring Kuwait in 1990, U.S. president George H. W. Bush feared that Iraqi president Saddam Hussein would use that triumph as a springboard to attack other nations in the region. So the Bush administration assembled an international coalition of nations and liberated Kuwait in 1991 in an operation known as Desert Storm. Although Bolk was trained and ready to deploy, she was not activated during that conflict. "I thought, I'm going to retire from the army and never go to war. This is just wrong," says Bolk.

While waiting for activation, Bolk continued to augment her education and advance her career. In 1987, she earned a certificate of public management from the School of Public and Environmental Affairs at Indiana University. The next year, she left Westview Hospital to become the director of nursing and surgical services at Winona Memorial Hospital in Indianapolis. In 1991, she obtained an MBA from Indiana Wesleyan University. Three years later, after a stint as a surgical services management consultant for D.J. Sullivan and Associates, she joined Curative Health Services Inc., where among other duties she was responsible for business expansion. She capped her education in 1996 with a bachelor's in nursing from Indiana Wesleyan.

Her public-service itch still not scratched, Bolk seized the chance for an international humanitarian adventure in 2002. An acquaintance who was a radiology sales representative mentioned that he was on his way to Ecuador to build homes for people who had leprosy. They were cured of the disease but were still ostracized by their communities because of missing body parts. She immediately volunteered to go along, and worked in a leper hospital for a week in the coastal city of Guayaquil. The experience was fulfilling. "I enjoyed working in a hospital with these wonderful people. They were the sweetest people," Bolk says.

Back on American soil, her career continued to progress thanks to her easygoing, confident management style, which hides a fierce determination and a razor focus—leadership capabilities that her next employer recognized. In 2004, she was hired to be chief operating officer at Kindred Healthcare Hospital in Indianapolis, a division of Kindred Healthcare Inc. She was tapped to be its next CEO when fate intervened.

According to the terms of the Middle East ceasefire brokered by the United Nations in 1991, Iraq—still led by Hussein—was forbidden to develop or possess weapons of mass destruction. Over the next decade, authorities continued to question whether Iraq had such weapons. Although Hussein denied it, much of the world, including U.S. president George W. Bush, did not believe him. That, coupled with Hussein's support of terrorism and his criminal treatment of Iraqi people, had the Bush administration readying America for war. On March 20, 2003, the United States launched the second invasion of Iraq, dubbed Operation Iraqi Freedom.

A little more than a month before the invasion, Bolk was finally mobilized—after eighteen years in the reserves. She was named acting commander of the 932nd Forward Surgical Team, which was attached to a special forces unit. Her team was responsible for performing life-saving surgery within earshot of the battlefield. Tapped to form the team she would lead, Bolk carefully selected from the pool of reservists personnel who had diverse abilities. Some built houses in civilian life; some were truck drivers or mechanics. That was not unusual. In the reserve units, 75 percent of the operating room technicians do not have careers in health care. Bolk also included a couple of farmers because, as she remembered from her years in Vincennes, "they can fix anything." Once she selected her team, the reservist nurses, medics, and physicians went through three months of intensive training. The unit strength was twenty soldiers: ten officers and ten enlisted men. She was the only woman.

Typically, surgeons rotated in and out of Iraq every ninety days; longer tours of duty could jeopardize their surgical practices. Bolk's tour of duty lasted five months, during which she was the only woman on the team and was believed to be the only woman among the five hundred service personnel within three hundred miles.

Life near the front lines doesn't bear much resemblance to the movie *MASH*, a 1970 comedy directed by Robert Altman (which inspired the hit TV series *M*A*S*H*) that depicted the exploits of medical teams in forward surgical units and combat support hospitals during the Korean War. Captains "Hawkeye" Pierce, "Trapper" John McIntyre, and "Duke" Forrest led a highly competent yet rollicking team in hi-jinks that only a good scriptwriter could dream up. Alcohol and sex were prevalent. In reality, what is referred to as General Order No. 1 prohibits alcohol consumption and sexual activities by U.S. Department of Defense personnel in a combat zone. Still, Bolk's 932nd was a close-knit, fun-loving group with a good share of jokesters—who followed General Order Number 1 most of the time. They constructed a nine-hole Frisbee golf course and generally enjoyed their limited leisure time—and each other. "I made friends. I made friends for life," says Bolk with a smile.

Five months of hazardous duty was exhilarating and certainly enough for most people, but not for her. Soon after Bolk returned home, she placed her name on the active duty volunteer list and in June 2006 was selected to serve as the head operating room nurse in charge of surgery on a team of sixteen people, this time men and women. Later that year, she was posted to Iraq with the 399th Combat Support Hospital for a fifteen-month tour of duty—three months in training and twelve months in action.

Bolk's two tours of duty in Iraq were quite dissimilar. In 2003, the United States fought Iraqi soldiers, but by 2006 the military faced attacks from insurgents, an armed, organized revolt against the Iraqi government and the U.S. occupation. The insurgents took hostages, deployed snipers, laid land mines, and employed other terrorist techniques, including suicide bombers who caused indiscriminate mass casualties—known as MASCAL in wartime shorthand. During her first tour of duty, Bolk set up her mobile unit within an eighth of a mile of the front, where actual shooting and killing were going on. In 2006, there was no front. Fighting occurred everywhere, a reality that presented different and horrific problems. Instead of wounds dealt by conventional arms, Bolk and her team had to handle the results of improvised explosive devices, some of them detonated on playgrounds. People came in with limbs blown off—sometimes dozens of patients at a time. Instead of dealing primarily with bullets, Bolk and her team removed ball bearings, dirt, glass, nails, bolts, screws, and pieces of rusty metal. The hospital treated a variety of patients, many of them American soldiers; however, the facility also cared for Iraqi police, Iraqi soldiers, insurgents, and civilians, including children. Bolk recalls treating a British journalist who had stepped on a land mine. The photographer with him was killed instantly. The journalist's foot was badly wounded. Bolk explains, "We put an external fixator on his ankle so he could be flown to England to make the decision with the counsel of his family, whether to remove his foot or go through years of multiple surgeries and physical therapy." That wasn't the worst of it. "The really hard wounds were when the snipers decided to get cute," Bolk says. "Instead of hitting people in the neck, they would hit them in the groin and take off their penises and testicles. The urologists sewed them back together the best they could."

More than halfway through her second tour of duty, Bolk's unit moved from Mosul to the western desert of Anbar Province and set up a thirty-bed hospital at Al Asad, the second largest air base. When the unit arrived and established the hospital, Anbar Province was being hit hard and was badly in need of a combat support hospital. The first American patients to arrive at the unit in Al Asad were an explosive detection team consisting of a dog and his handler who were blown up by an improvised explosive device (IED). The handler did not make it. The medical team patched up the dog, whose rear flank was torn up. "You have to know how to do all kinds of things," shrugs Bolk. Mass casualties became routine. Patients usually came in four at a time because that was the helicopter ambulance's capacity. Often four patients were in the operating room while four more were being triaged outside, waiting to go to surgery.

As a soldier, Bolk makes no comment on the political issues that led to the conflict. "We're here to do our job. Whether the leader is right or wrong, we've got a job to do," she explains. Her team's job was to surgically stabilize patients before shipping them off to larger hospitals where they could receive specialized care—stop the bleeding, try to save limbs, and amputate when absolutely necessary. Bolk gives credit to the battlefield medics and wounded soldiers' battle buddies who are present right when injuries occur. One of the best things the United States has done for its soldiers is to prepare them to treat injuries immediately, she says. If a soldier is wounded, a buddy will slap on a tourniquet to save him from bleeding to death, a simple solution that was not thought of in previous wars. "We didn't even do that in my first tour of duty in 2003," Bolk says. "It sounds so simple. The tourniquet has saved lots of lives."

Bolk often wonders what became of some of the military personnel she has treated. She remembers specifically a marine who was hurt so badly his survival defied everyone's expectations. He was brought to surgery more than once and took more than fifty units of blood—enough to replenish his entire blood supply three times over. He was airlifted from Al Asad to Germany. Bolk found out that he has since recovered, physically, at least. Can anybody, including Bolk, be the same after experiences like these? Bolk was affected like most of the others. "We had been working in Iraq ten months. The one event that really got me the most was a MASCAL on Mother's Day. We had people coming in all blown up and you wondered at the futility of it all. Does it help the cause of the insurgents to blow up children? Will it ever end? I cried."

In May 2007, Bolk, a lieutenant colonel, was selected for the U.S. Army War College, a prestigious training center located in Carlisle, Pennsylvania, on the five hundred–acre campus of the historic Carlisle Barracks. The college has trained nearly all of this country's elite military leaders since its establishment in 1901, including General H. Norman Schwarzkopf, commander of U.S. forces in Operation Desert Shield. Bolk's class consists of active and reserve officers in all branches of the U.S. military, as well as a few military leaders from allied countries and civilians who work for the government. Bolk must engage in an intensive distance education program throughout the year and spend two weeks on campus in the summers of 2008 and 2009. It is a fast-paced curriculum, and the attrition rate is estimated to be 50 percent. Acceptance in the War College is evidence that her superiors deem Bolk worthy of promotion. Naturally, she hopes to be promoted to full colonel.

At the time of her second call-up, Bolk was transitioning into the CEO position of Kindred Hospital. By law, the hospital corporation is obligated to offer her a similar position upon her return. Although no such job is available in Indiana, Kindred Healthcare has operations in more than five hundred locations in thirty-nine states. Bolk has no desire to leave Indiana, however. "I am a Hoosier through and through, so I'll have to find something else to do. Maybe it won't be in health care. Maybe it will be something else," she says. Bolk certainly has the talent, education, and self-confidence to excel in any field that appeals to her.

Outside of work, Bolk is a private pilot aspiring to obtain a seaplane rating. She also is a scuba diver, loves rollerblading, and is very serious about maintaining the physical requirements necessary for active duty. To accomplish that, she must pass a physical fitness test every six months that includes sit-ups, push-ups, and a two-mile run. For a perfect score, she must perform at least 34 push-ups, 66 sit-ups, and run 2 miles in less than 17 minutes, 36 seconds. Bolk is confident she can pass the next test, but she's not aiming for perfection. Although she has not made time for marriage, Bolk would like to be a grandmother. "All I have to do is find a husband who already has grandchildren," she laughs.

With more than twenty years of service in the reserves, Bolk is eligible for retirement. She is not interested: "They will have to kick me out." If that happens—or she has a change of heart and does retire—Bolk figures she might join the Peace Corps for a couple years, "just to see how much more is out there."

For now, though, she wouldn't mind reactivating, perhaps serving in Afghanistan. Although there may be some repercussions. "My mother has already told me that she is not too old to bend me over her knee if I do this again," Bolk says with a broad smile.

"I love Indiana. I love America, but young women ought to see the world from a different perspective," she says. Bolk also advises young women to do great work in school—to engage in extracurricular activities and be competitive in sports because that will build confidence for competing in the business world. "Do something wild. Go out there and see the world."

If she stays put, Bolk undoubtedly would be called to duty in the event of a wartime disaster in America. Until that time, she continues on reserve status—serving one weekend a month and two weeks in the summer. In 2008, she served as executive officer of the 307th Medical Group based in Columbus, Ohio. It was comprised of more than fifteen hundred reserve soldiers from Ohio, Indiana, and Illinois, covering sixteen subordinate units including two battalion-size combat support hospitals.

Bolk is active in the Indianapolis Kiwanis Club, where she has earned awards including the Citizen Soldier Award in 2003 and the Kiwanian of the Year in 2007. In 2005, she was recognized by Senator Richard Lugar for excellence in public service.

As a young Hoosier, Mary Bolk decided she wasn't making enough of a difference, so she risked her life in the service of her country. She ended up saving lives, living out her ambition to become a modern-day Florence Nightingale who can look back and say, "I did make a difference."

Nancy Noël

A Portrait of
Beauty and Grace

*Y*our daughter, Nancy, is not mentally capable of completing satisfactory work here at Immaculate Heart of Mary Elementary School. Perhaps you should send her to Noble School. They are especially equipped to deal with children who are mentally challenged."

In the Noël family, academic achievement was expected. Nancy's father and two brothers were Cornell graduates. Her sister attended Cornell and an uncle has a Harvard degree. "I was the second of six children and the minute we were hatched our parents were trying to decide what university we were going to attend. In a family where everyone excelled, I was a disappointment," this third-generation Hoosier explains with a touch of irony. Twenty-five years after the Indianapolis elementary school teacher quoted above gave up on her, Noël had established herself as an internationally famous artist, achieving far greater success than anyone in that remarkable family could have imagined.

★ ★ ★

Born October 25, 1945, Noël knew she was intelligent but felt adults could not understand how her mind worked. Today it would not be difficult to diagnosis Noël's learning problem as dyslexia, a type of disability that makes it difficult for some people to read and spell. That does not mean that people with dyslexia lack intelligence. In fact, dyslexic

subjects tend to score significantly higher than their peers on tests of creativity, memory, and reasoning. There is no cure for the disorder, but certain techniques can help subjects overcome some of the symptoms. It just takes practice.

Noël's inefficiency in processing written language threatened her self-esteem. Perhaps that is the reason her demeanor today is considered by some to be aloof. She isn't. Noël is genuinely modest and shy. When that barrier is broken, she is personable and warm. She is also bright and articulate. As a child, Noël sought refuge with animals. "Animals don't judge you," a fully confident Noël adds while explaining her childhood frustration. "I was always running off to find a horse to ride." She won many ribbons jumping and showing horses. She also found solace in athletics, becoming an excellent skier and sailor.

Noël's fascination and love for animals has endured, infusing her personal and professional lives. Much of her artwork features likenesses of cows, dogs, cats, sheep, rabbits, mice, and other animals. Noël also shares her Zionsville, Indiana, home and ample estate with a dozen geese, twenty llamas, three dogs, ten cats, and three horses. A rehab license Noël shares with others enables her to care for abandoned wild animals, including fifteen raccoons she has raised and returned to the wild. Caring for these animals was a formative project when her two sons were growing up and a rewarding experience for the entire family.

Noël's immense creative talent should not have been difficult to predict, given her family history. Her grandfathers were engineers and inventors at Eli Lilly and Company, the Indianapolis pharmaceutical company. Her maternal grandfather, William A. Hanley, a member of the Lilly board of directors, was instrumental in developing the process that allowed gelatin capsules to be mass produced rather than manufactured by hand. As a result, the Lilly factory produced 2.5 million capsules a day without the touch of a human hand—a magnificent achievement in 1917. Noël's mother, Louise Hanley, was a singer who curtailed her career aspirations in order to marry Harry Jerome Noël, an air force veteran who loved music. Although he was disqualified from pilot training because he was colorblind, Harry could appreciate the subtle nuances in his daughter's paintings and was proud of her accomplishments. Although Noël is the only professional artist in the family, her brother Bill inherited some of the artistic talent. He is a flutist, albeit an amateur. Family lore holds that Noël's great grandmother Molly McGrath was a brilliant artist, although none of her work has survived. One of the few photographs of Grandmother Molly shows her on a motorcycle at the approximate age of 99. Perhaps Noël derives her adventurous spirit from Molly.

Noël's talent as an artist was recognized in elementary school and although she never achieved above a C in math, English, or science, her art projects were on the blackboard for parents to admire on Back to School Night. Noël muddled through her primary grades parrying comments from her teachers that she was lazy or just not all there. Her parents were not convinced. They saw some promise and provided her with private art lessons from a woman in her neighborhood, Ruth Kothe, an accomplished artist. Noël's confidence began to rebound. One of the Noël/Kothe collaborations hangs in her studio as a testimony to this early mentor who was one of the first to recognize Noël's talent.

While in high school, Noël participated in an Indianapolis Symphony Orchestra contest requiring children to paint their interpretation of a selection from a symphony. Noël won an award in that competition, and her work was exhibited at Butler University's Clowes Memorial Hall. Her parents took her to Clowes and she wandered down the hall looking at all the entries, but she could not find hers. It was the last picture at the end of the hall—and it was framed. "It made me feel like all of a sudden I could do something. I could compete in some way. I could be somebody," Noël recalls. After enduring two years of her sub-par performance in public high school, Noël's parents made a desperate attempt to educate their daughter to the level expected, shipping her off to St. Mary's Preparatory School at Notre Dame. While at St. Mary's, she began to sell her paintings.

After high school, Noël enrolled at the College of Mount St. Joseph in Cincinnati, Ohio. Mount St. Joseph was primarily a nursing school, but it also offered a highly reputable arts program. Referred to by its students as the Mount, the college is known for personal attention and support. With practice, Noël learned to compensate for her dyslexia. She took classes in theology, physiology, and art and graduated with honors. Years later, Mount St. Joseph presented Noël an award recognizing her high achievement.

In 1967, while Noël was in her early 20s, she was asked to work as a portrait artist at the first Penrod Arts Fair in Indianapolis. Still held each year on the first Saturday after Labor Day, the fair attracts more than thirty thousand people to the grounds of the Indianapolis Museum of Art. Proceeds provide grants for Indianapolis-area charitable organizations. The Penrod name is taken from Indianapolis native Booth Tarkington's character Penrod Schofield in the book *Penrod, His Complete Story*. Penrod was known for boyish high energy and inventiveness. To him, school was merely a state of confinement. In that respect, Noël and the fictional Penrod would have been a perfect match. Noël labored at the fair for a few years, enjoying her afternoons in the expansive park setting of the museum grounds as she helped the cause.

Even in its early years, the Penrod Arts Fair attracted reputable artists and generated thousands of dollars in sales. Lacking a reputation, Noël was an inexpensive alternative. She was asked to paint portraits for $2 apiece. Because her work was of such high quality, people waited in the hot summer sun for hours. Even at dusk, while other artists were packing up their exhibits, her customers remained in the fading light hoping to see their likeness on a Noël canvas. Some would-be customers who didn't make it before dark requested a separate appointment. And thus Noël's independent portrait business began. Portraits she used to create for $2 now command a minimum of $40,000. There is a two-year waiting list at that price.

In the late 1960s, although Noël sold a few of her paintings for modest prices, her family maintained the hope that she could do something more substantial with her life. Noël was desperate to prove that she could be a success, but her career choices were limited. Because she was dyslexic, a profession involving heavy reading was impossible. So in 1970, Noël purchased a house in Broad Ripple, a section of Indianapolis popular with artists and young people, and renovated it for an art gallery. The gallery sold works of other artists and a few Noël originals. In December 1976, the 31-year-old Noël married, sold the gallery, and began to paint in earnest. Because she had painted under the name Noël for so long, she retained her maiden name. Her productivity escalated and her prices followed suit.

The Noël national reputation took on an additional glow in 1991, when Churchill Downs, Inc. commissioned Noël to paint the program for the 117th running of the Kentucky Derby. From that original oil painting, titled *Odds On*, posters and prints were made and sold to collectors throughout the United States. General H. Norman Schwarzkopf, who led Allied troops to victory in Operation Desert Storm, was the grand marshal, but the day belonged to Derby winner Strike the Gold and to Noël—the honored guest. Her success at the Kentucky Derby was followed by requests from other sporting events including the Pan American Games.

Noël had honed her artistic skills while in college, working part-time painting reproductions of great works for a dealer who in time disappeared without paying for a number of Noël's efforts. No doubt the experience helped Noël sharpen her business skills, too. She learned the painful lesson that not everyone can be trusted in the art world—something Noël has been reminded of over the years as she and her work have become increasingly popular. Now all of Noël's works are copyrighted with the National Registry practically before the paint is dry. Despite that protection, thieves have illegally sold many of her prints, particularly through the internet. The latest printing processes are so professional that the fakes often are difficult to discern from the originals. In an effort to curtail this theft, Noël has eliminated much of her distribution network and runs that aspect of her operation from the "Sanctuary," her office on Zionsville's Main Street, with help from longtime assistants Jane Jimison and Kathy Pierle.

Established as a church in 1854, the Sanctuary was sold to an antique store, then to a furniture store before descending into disuse and disrepair. When Noël purchased it in August 2005, the church was like Charles Dickens's Miss Haversham, a jilted lady that time had forgotten. The demanding renovation and design process, including construction of a twenty-five-foot fireplace and a hand-carved staircase, took almost a year and cost more than $1 million—more than twice the original estimate. Noël has no regrets, though. Restored to grandeur beyond the vision of its original architect, the church has once again become a place of peace and comfort. In the basement, a crew busily fulfills print orders from around the world while fans mill about on the first floor, drawn from as far away as New York, California, and Alaska to purchase prints, limited editions, and original artwork literally right off the church walls. On weekends, as many as five thousand admirers may pass through the Sanctuary and be greeted by the angel "Destiny," depicted in a large Noël original oil on canvas of the same name.

As an adolescent with challenges, Noël just "tried to put one foot in front of the other." Today, Noël—an attractive blond whose pleasant smile would fit nicely on one of her own canvases of beautiful people—is thinking longer range. She looks forward to time in her studio as her life's passion. "I have been the most successful in my life when I have worried the least," she says. "I don't worry about making money or anything else, I only try to do what I do best."

Noël's studio is located on the second floor of a French blue-green barn on her Zionsville estate. After climbing a steep flight of steps, one is reminded of Santa's workshop. Benches, tables, and counters hold an abundance of artist supplies and equipment, including easels, brushes, and research photographs. And then there is the paint, tubes and tubes of paint—some exhausted, from which very little can be squeezed, and others bursting with opportunity—all without caps. Although the paint is strewn about the studio and piled in bins like fallen bowling pins,

Noël is careful and organized with her brushes, many made from the finest sable. Competent in all mediums, Noël loves acrylics but mainly uses oil paints. Like an athlete in a zone, she may paint every day for six weeks and then not climb the studio stairs for several weeks, depending upon her disposition and inspiration.

Noël's studio is illuminated through large windows allowing a northeast exposure, considered ideal for painting. Overhead lighting is available for dreary days and nighttime work. Ideas abound. The studio walls are covered with work-in-progress canvases, including a painting Noël did in high school that she is revisiting. In the main workspace hangs a large acrylic painting of an elk. This commissioned piece took Noël to Utah, where she spent three winter days photographing elk before deciding to paint an animal with a five-foot antler span. Noël uses digital photography to help remember the detail, angles, and attitude of her subjects that will be shown on the final canvas. The acrylic elk is awash in color, but if Noël finishes it in oil much of the surreal look will give way to a natural depiction.

Noël's work has taken her to Africa and England, to mountains and oceans, to the Indianapolis 500, and into the homes of celebrities. But Noël's success as an artist also has enhanced her opportunities to help others. As she achieved more, her contributions to not-for-profit institutions escalated. "When I do something nice for somebody, it always comes back to me a hundred-fold," she says. In 2000, while vacationing near Lake Victoria in Kenya and searching for children to paint, she was escorted by Kenyan friends to a preschool, a one-room hut filled with about sixty children between the ages of 3 and 6. The guests listened for a moment to children buzzing in their native language before the teacher, a young woman of the Lau tribe, introduced herself as Mrs. Tom and welcomed Noël to the school. After Noël spent some time with the children taking photographs, Mrs. Tom announced, "You are our first visitor, so we would like to name the school after you." Noël responded by pledging her support to the school, now known as the N.A. Noël Preschool.

"When you say you're going to do something, you must do it," she advises. Noël kept her promise. With her financial support, the school in the fishing village of Mbita has expanded from one hut to three large classrooms where about two hundred students are educated daily from mid-day to just before dark. Although Noël provides for the needs of these children, including medical expenses, she has not created a formal organization or foundation to handle the details. When Noël visits, the children call her "Mum."

Children are very important to Noël, who has two sons of her own. Alexander Noël Kosene is a writer who enjoys art and Michael Noël Kosene is a businessman associated with his father as a commercial real estate developer.

Perhaps because of her difficulties when growing up, Noël remains especially sensitive to the suffering of others. She often herds her llamas into a trailer and accompanies them on goodwill missions to nursing homes and hospices throughout Indiana. Her llamas also provide comfort for special-needs children and groups from the Indiana School for the Blind and Brooke's Place, an organization that assists children whose siblings or other family members have died. Noël believes that a child, even when in a coma, can sense a difference when a llama enters into the room. "I have seen a drastic change in the monitor as a llama approaches the bedside," says Noël. When Noël and her llamas visited a housing complex for senior citizens, a resident who had been in a deeply depressed mental state—not speaking or showing any emotion for some time—became animated. According to Noël, caregivers often remark about the dramatic effect that llamas have on patients. The llamas are remarkably sensitive and calming. They are also housebroken, an unusual trait that makes them particularly appropriate for indoor visits.

Noël also is generous with her art. Weekly, through the donations of her prints, Noël supports a number of Indianapolis charitable institutions. She has worked with charities to designate original paintings to be published as prints, then allocates a portion of the proceeds from sales of the prints to the organization. Her "hands-on" philanthropic work includes the women's prison, family support centers for abused children, and various animal protection societies.

Like the work of many famous artists, much of Noël's art can be categorized by phases. Noël jokes that her well-known Amish, African, and Angel pieces demonstrate that she is on the A's and has not yet gotten to the B's. Noël said there is a story behind every painting. The extraordinarily successful Angel series, for example, was prompted by the death of her horse, a large white Arabian named El Kader, meaning "the powerful one." That love also sparked Noël's best-selling book, *All God's Creatures Go to Heaven*, which depicts heaven as a place of reunion for all living creatures.

The Angel series evoked a curious reaction among her fans. "People approached me, wondering if I see angels and sharing stories about their own angel experiences," she says. But Noël is quick to point out that "religion is not part of me and I make that very clear. Religion has nothing to do with what I do." She is spiritual, but takes issue with organized religion despite being raised Catholic. One of her missions is to try to help people understand that they have mistakenly humanized God. "Most Christians think that God looks like Jesus, lives in the clouds, and is quick to judge our day-to-day affairs. That is bizarre to me. Even as a little girl sitting in church, I thought little of what I was led to believe made any sense. Too often, religion undermines a person's intuition when seeking truth and spirituality."

Noël derives her inspiration from experience. Her Africa phase is characterized by big colorful paintings of people of the Hararo tribe, whom she encountered during a trip there. Missionaries taught the Hararos their present form of dress, and they wear large hats and big bouffant dresses in vibrant colors. She later painted members of other tribes, including the Samburu and Maasai. All the paintings in the African series have been sold except three that she put aside for her sons.

In 1986, in an effort to study figure and composition, Noël decided to paint the Amish. She traveled to Shipshewana, a rural town in northern Indiana known for its traditional Amish communities. On her first visit, Noël arrived by helicopter and caused quite a stir in the community. Amused, the Amish not only helped Noël with her studies, but eventually gave her permission to photograph and paint their children, a privilege seldom granted. Noël stayed with an Amish family for a few days, awakening with the children to watch them milk the herd before school. What began as a simple endeavor to paint Amish children morphed into the series—one of Noël's most popular efforts. The print of her *Sarah* painting is Noël's best seller, with over a half million sold.

Noël prints continue to sell to a growing number of collectors. In addition to her regular reproductions, Noël creates state-of-the-art giclée prints, very much like paintings themselves. From the French word meaning "spurt," giclée prints are produced one at a time, using a process in which ink saturates the canvas. Noël's original work has sold for as much as $130,000, whereas the giclée prints could sell for $200 to $2,000. Noël's original works sell briskly and are avidly collected by her fans, including Oprah Winfrey, Maya Angelou, and Jane Seymour.

Noël also has published eight books, including a children's book and an illustrated cookbook, co-authored by her assistant Donna Deardorff. The combined sale of more than 250,000 books seems a fitting—if ironic—tribute to a woman who had trouble reading. She continues to write. "Do not limit yourself—that's the curse," she warns. "If you limit yourself out of fear, then you can't do anything else. I did that for a long time and now I know my future is uncertain but unlimited."

Still cautiously putting one foot in front of the other, Nancy Noël has successfully challenged the limitations imposed by dyslexia and turned it around to do what others cannot. Along the way, this lady of beauty and grace has established herself among the truly great Indiana artists.

Becky Skillman

―――☆―――

Good Neighbor,
Determined Leader

She entered politics in a county where most elected officials were men. That didn't daunt her. She ran for office at an age when most people are still trying to find themselves. She knew what she wanted. She had a husband and son to care for—and she did. She didn't have a college degree, and almost everyone who achieved anything in Indiana politics did. That didn't matter. She told herself she had a job she wanted to do, set out to do it, and never stopped until she reached her goal. She is Indiana's Lieutenant Governor Becky Skillman.

Skillman can be called single-minded. From the time she was a child, she has been fascinated by the world of politics. Her grandfather, Edmund Flinn, talked to her as if she were an adult about elected officials like Senator Bill Jenner and Congressman Earl Wilson, about affairs in Washington, D.C., about why it was important to follow the philosophy of the Republican Party. Hailing from a Lawrence County pioneer family, he was a down-to-earth man who worked for Stone City Construction, helping to build roads.

"He blasted tunnels, all of those cuts through the limestone territory that became Highway 37. It was very dangerous work," Skillman says. "He never graduated from high school, but he was exceptionally wise. When my grandfather was 86 and I was in the senate, he'd call me on a weekly basis to quiz me, to see if I knew what was going on in California

or Texas or Florida. 'Grandfather,' I'd say, 'you have all day to watch TV and read the newspapers. We are a bit busy up here.'"

Indeed, she has been busy from the time she was Becky Fodrill in grade school near Bedford. "My mother always said I was serious," she concedes. "I thought about things many other girls weren't interested in." She did well in school, enjoying everything from science and art to home economics. "My husband chuckles because I won the Betty Crocker Homemaker Award as the top high school student in Home Ec. Now I rarely have time to cook at home."

As a teenager, she involved herself in typical hometown activities like 4-H and some not-so-typical pastimes—at least for a girl—like drag racing and playing the drums. "I inherited my father's passion for cars," admits Skillman, "and I loved to street race with the boys. We would drive very fast through the country. My nickname in high school was 'Hot Rod.' At night, we found strips on state highways to compete." She was the only female hot rod in Bedford. She also formed a rock band that played concerts at school functions. When rock bands came into the National Guard Armory for dances on Saturday night, Skillman often was asked to play a set. As recently as 2000, when she was at an event in Washington County—one of the five counties that she represented as a state senator—she sat in with a local band.

Glamour came naturally to the slim blond with a warm personality. She was 1968 Homecoming Queen at Tunnelton High, receiving her tiara during the biggest basketball game of the season. She remembers walking into the gym on the arm of the "favorite fellow of the day" and viewing the game from a throne on the stage.

A high school highlight for her was Girls' State, a week-long crash course in politics and government. Each year, the American Legion Auxiliary assembles rising high school seniors from throughout Indiana to learn firsthand how government operates. Many Hoosier achievers have had their start in Boys' or Girls' State, and her experience was no different. "I was a Girls' State delegate in the year in which we chose Jane Pauley as the governor. Eight hundred girls had traveled from all over Indiana to come to the event. Since it was held at Indiana University, I was only twenty miles from home. I ran for county council and I won.

"The American Legion Auxiliary makes the experience as authentic as they possibly can. Candidates are required to campaign, with well-developed platforms. My mother would say that is what piqued my interest in politics, and yet I already had an interest stimulated by my grandfather."

Still, Girls' State honed that interest and helped her discover what would become one of the platforms of her career and life. It was not the thrill of the "game," the triumph of winning and being recognized that mattered—it was the honor of serving. "I am deeply affected by what being in office means. When I took my first job for the county, walking into that courthouse in the middle of the square, I was filled with emotion. And then, to enter that first day in the Indiana Statehouse built right after the Civil War—with the busts of famous Hoosiers all around . . . it was a sense of understanding your place in a history that had been going on for quite a long time." The experience also delivered a sense that "you were in a position to do things—to help your friends and neighbors."

Getting to that point took a big leap of faith. After graduating from high school in 1968, she and her best friend Jane Clampitt decided to work for the summer and then go to Purdue. Skillman landed a dental assistant position, learning on the job. "It was interesting work and the pay was quite a bit better than that of most of the people in my age group in Bedford," she says. "I stayed on for three years, just immersed in the job and happy." Clampitt, meanwhile, attended Purdue without her.

Skillman was lured away from that job by the promise of public service—this time at the county courthouse, where the county recorder was looking for a chief deputy. Skillman signed on, after promising the recorder she "wouldn't tell anyone I wasn't 21 yet." She was 20—not old enough to vote at the time—when she entered the world of record-keeping in a quiet, sometimes dusty and hot old building. She sorted through deeds, mortgages, liens, and records from cemetery plots. "Everything had to be recorded by hand—no computers back then. Our office had one of the few microfilm capabilities in the state, and that did help. Once a week, we'd microfilm all of those documents and send the tape off. . . . But it gave me the opportunity to really help people. You can truly answer anyone's questions about a deed, a mortgage, or military discharge. . . . I could make everybody happy." That wouldn't last forever.

The county recorder couldn't run for re-election after two terms in office and although she was just 25, Skillman thought she could handle the job. So she ran, and no one challenged her in the primary. She had an opponent in the 1976 general election, but Lawrence County was a traditional Republican stronghold—perhaps giving her the courage to take the plunge. Still, that first race was strenuous. Skillman tried several "startling" things new to Lawrence County, designing her own newspaper ads (TV political advertising wasn't popular yet) with catchy photographs and exciting text and headlines, for example. She ran against an older real estate agent who was well known in Bedford. "Her prominence could have been used against me, but the other real estate agents rallied to my cause," she recalls. "They didn't want a competitor in that office which had as its duty the recording of deeds."

Along the way, she began to see the fish bowl she would be entering if she devoted her life to politics. It was slightly uncomfortable wondering if the townspeople she saw on the street knew who she was from the photos in the paper. Picnics and pitch-in suppers with a lengthy list of Republican candidates all wanting to have their say became part of her routine. Her mother expressed doubts. Democrat Jimmy Carter was running for president and seemed to be doing well. "Mother," Skillman told her, "You know Lawrence County from the get-go has been Republican. I won't lose." And she didn't. She walked in those hundred-year-old doors with a new sense of reverence, returning to the office she'd worked in as its boss.

Serving the public wasn't the only thing Skillman had to do in those days of the 1970s. She had married her high school sweetheart and built a home. Steve Skillman was 16 years old when he asked 12-year-old Becky for a date. "Mother, of course, said no," she recalls. "Finally, we had our first date when I was 15. He called me princess—and still does—and I fell in love." They were married when she was 19. When her only child, Aaron, was born in 1979, Skillman already was a seasoned public servant.

"One of the real challenges to women in public office is family life. I was blessed in those days when Aaron was a baby because my family became his babysitters. His first caretaker was my grandmother, who was still in her 60s when he was born. She came to our home, and I was only five minutes away," Skillman says. "I could run home if there was a need, and as he grew up, he came to the courthouse. I have memories of him sliding down the banister from the third to the second floor."

She served two four-year terms as county recorder, then ran for county clerk, a position she held from 1985 to 1992. While she was county clerk, Skillman was elected by her statewide peers to be president of the Association of Indiana Counties, a position that required her to lobby the Indiana General Assembly. In 1992, she ran for the Indiana senate. After another passionate and anxious campaign, Skillman found she soon would be sitting in the formal senate chamber, where it takes an eternity to walk to the podium. But none of the other obstacles had stopped her in any way. Bring on the challenge of legislative service.

Leaving Bedford behind, she made the seventy-five-mile commute to Indianapolis, parked, and climbed the statehouse steps. The same sense of elation and awe struck her as she walked across the tile in that large, silent, almost tomb-like lobby under a capitol dome that seemed to float above the city. She brought boxes in, moved into a cubicle office, and awaited the opening of the senate. "I thought, Grandfather was born in 1907. It was hard for him to think of his granddaughter, a southern Indiana girl, even driving to Indianapolis, let alone taking up a seat in the senate."

What she found was a far cry from the orderly governmental pattern of the county offices she had left. State legislators seemed to move slowly, taking the days as they came and extemporizing solutions on the fly. There was no time management. "Mothers and competent women who work have had to organize their time, make lists of things to do, juggle responsibilities. The session started very slowly and only at the end of it were major decisions made, bills passed. And to add to the difficulties, we were linked with the House of Representatives. If they did not come to meet on a certain day, we had to 'burn that day' also. Days were wasted." Something would have to be done about that. Eventually, after encouragement from Skillman and other newer members of the senate, the two bodies' schedules were divorced. As long as the senate ended on the same day as the house, each group could operate on its own. It was a big improvement.

Her first year in the general assembly was eventful. "We were at a budget impasse, ran a special session at the end, worked throughout the entire month of June until the night before state government would have shut down, the final day before a new fiscal year would start." Although the session seemed tough, Skillman did not have the perspective to know it was more demanding than usual. "When other years came that were much less busy, I saw that my freshman year had been grueling and unusual," she says. Still, she was impressed by the variety of interests, varying levels of economic need, and different geographic makeup of her legislative peers. "They came at legislative action in a different way, too," she says. "Some were used to rough-and-tumble politics, used to employing strong-arm tactics; some were more indirect. Each found a way to represent his or her district and the people in that district."

Even as she unpacked photos from home, Skillman worried about her son and husband—at least at first. "I had been only five minutes away from Aaron, able to run in with cupcakes as a room mother, take him and his friends to the opera, or see their performances. I was calling from my new office three or four times a day." Finally the 13-year-old said to her, "Mother, you're too concerned. We're fine here." For Steve and Aaron, life in their familiar surroundings seemed not too different from what it had been. For Senator Becky Skillman, Bedford seemed a long way away.

"Often they came up to the capitol, of course. I wanted Aaron to feel as comfortable in the statehouse as he had in the county courthouse," she says. "But I had to re-think that when he followed some interns on their rite-of-passage trip out onto the catwalk around the statehouse dome." The family and Skillman adjusted, and she plunged into that first legislative session, then the others that followed. "I only wanted to serve."

To that end, she championed causes early on—including an initiative designed to encourage economic success in small towns and rural areas. "Three of the five counties I represented were declared 'distressed counties.' That meant that their unemployment rate was 2 percent above the state average for at least a two-year period of time," she recalls. These little towns and the areas around them needed help. She passed legislation enabling businesses that expanded or located in one of these distressed counties to recoup the taxes they would pay, and roll that money back into an economic development project.

She was surprised to discover Indiana had no development strategy for rural counties. At her urging, the legislature requested that state officials submit such a strategy, but the first report was nothing more than a statistical summary—nothing that would point to action for better times. And there was little funding. It was only a start.

As she worked on building support for the rural development initiative, Skillman's talents as a conciliator came in handy. "I discovered an interesting situation in the senate: The splits which occurred were not always between Republicans and Democrats but just as often between rural senators and those from urban areas. Urban-area state senators didn't always feel the closeness we in small towns experienced with our constituents. I felt personally responsible when I saw my people on the streets in my area, sometimes struggling to make a living. They came to me and expected me to do something to help them." Being able to do that—to spur the rural economic initiative—would mean she would have to cross the aisle. That wasn't as difficult as it might sound.

"I like people. I was in southern Indiana and most of the legislators I served with from that area were from the Democratic Party. I wanted to work with them and enjoyed the camaraderie and satisfaction of putting something together that would help the area we all cared about and represented. I was more concerned about getting things right than who has the pride of authorship of the bill signed into law."

She has a list of senate achievements of which she is proud, including local government participation in energy-saving contracts. After hearing about the rising cost of energy bills from local government and university representatives, Skillman authored legislation to ensure that their bills would decrease if they installed energy-saving devices. She also championed a law that removes some of the red tape and bureaucracy that complicated Indiana's adoption process, as well as legislation that gives counties full-time prosecuting attorneys. Before that bill passed, many counties faced conflicts of interest as part-time prosecuting attorneys balanced their county responsibilities with full-time legal careers outside the courthouse.

In 2004, she was running again for the senate, still unopposed in the primary. She was happy with where she was, holding the No. 2 leadership position in the senate. Her son had long since attended college and was on his own, and her husband, who had retired from factory management at General Motors, was continuing to support her in her lifetime work. She even had returned to school at Indiana Wesleyan University, where she completed two years toward her bachelor's degree. Then the call came to serve in another capacity. She had been an unofficial adviser to gubernatorial hopeful Mitch Daniels for about ten months, and he was starting to look for a running mate. "It was logical that he would turn to leadership in the senate, leadership in the house, and long-time political allies to help him. We had regular contact but we did not discuss specifics of the fall race. It was after the primary, when he was sure he was the candidate, that he began an intensive search."

She knew she might be considered. Friends had told her they had suggested her name to the Republican candidate. "I heard there were one hundred names on the list. I truly wasn't putting myself out there because I wanted events to unfold as they should, in logical time and order. In my heart I knew he was the right man for Indiana. That's what made it so terribly exciting when I was chosen—being part of a team, having the opportunity to make a real difference in the lives of Hoosiers."

Even so, the timing gave her pause. Everything was settled and satisfying in the senate position she had held for twelve years. Her work and friends and future all seemed so steady. And although Kathy Davis became the state's first female lieutenant governor when Joe Kernan took over following the death of Governor Frank O'Bannon, no woman had been elected to the job. Still, "I gave up my senate seat, my leadership position, and my advantage in being unopposed, when the Republican State Convention confirmed my nomination in June."

She never saw gender as an issue in their victory, but Skillman understood she was making strides in a field that still was predominantly male. "If I am considered a role model for today's young women, that's a great honor. I aim to live each day accordingly." The election win sent the new state leaders to large, busy offices in the statehouse. Skillman brought her southern Indiana–inspired interest in the rural development initiative with her. Continuing to help small towns—and their residents—was high on her agenda. As lieutenant governor, she and her staff founded the Office of Community and Rural Affairs to focus on Indiana's small towns and rural areas. It won legislative approval in 2005, after 650 individuals from around the state offered input into the process of improving rural Indiana. It was another nonpartisan effort that called for compromise and conciliation.

Her ability to successfully navigate party lines was even more apparent in the effort to save southern Indiana's Crane Naval Surface Warfare

Center, which the federal government proposed closing in 2005. State leaders got involved, making the case to keep the military installation, which employed several thousand engineers, scientists, and technicians.

"If anyone would have told me that I would be spending so much time at the Pentagon, I wouldn't have believed it," Skillman says. She and the governor assembled a team from many involved groups: the former base director, concerned citizens, both political parties, and state and local government. Former senator Dan Coats became the effort's lobbyist. Still, "the Department of Defense was interested in only one thing: the best military value of these bases. You can go to them and complain that jobs will be lost or that the base is an economic hub; they don't care about that. That meant we had to work hard to present the state's position." The base ultimately was not closed, and Skillman proudly points to a football in her office signed by grateful people in the Crane area. "They called me their quarterback," she says.

These days, when she's not running around in a golf cart at the State Fair sampling frozen Pepsi and touting the many fine qualities of corn, the lieutenant governor may be entertaining the Guatemalan ambassador who wants to discuss the growth of trade between the state and his country. Some call her Indiana's goodwill ambassador, touting the state's strengths to foreign dignitaries. Skillman also has gone abroad herself, leading missions to improve trade with places like Central America, Taiwan, and Vietnam.

At a biotechnology center in Taiwan where meetings were to be held, her nameplate read "Mr. Becky Skillman." Noticing the discrepancy, the CEO of the trade center approached her. "YOU are the lieutenant governor?" he asked, seemingly astonished, and apologized for the mistake. "Not everyone expects to find women as active in business and government as we are," Skillman says. That's especially true when the woman in question still looks like a prom queen.

The Indiana delegation she led to Vietnam was one of the first to visit Ho Chi Minh City. It was a real experience for someone from Bedford —or anywhere else, for that matter. "We didn't know what to expect. It all had exciting possibilities: Sixty percent of the population in Vietnam is under 30, many young professionals. We didn't realize they had been advertising our visit for weeks, believing it would enhance the esteem of the regime. As we stepped down from the van, it was onto a real red carpet."

Skillman hopes to continue her duties as lieutenant governor in a second term. Governor Daniels is thrilled with that decision. "Some women are almost too cute and sweet for their own good, because people tend to underestimate them. As endearing a person as she is, no one should ever underestimate Becky," he said. "She is a full partner in our administration, my No. 1 confidant, counselor, and sounding board. And when it comes to dealing with the legislature, she leads me."

When asked her plans following another term in office, Skillman responded coyly. "If in politics a week is a year, five years from now feels like an eternity and I'm not sure how you make such a decision until it's time to make the decision." Still, she would like to continue serving the state. "It's been an amazing opportunity in which to make a difference. It's provided so many experiences. I am proud of all the accomplishments. My most special memories will be about the people of our state, their strength, their courage, and their character," Skillman says.

Strength, courage, and character—add a strong competitive spirit and that's an apt description of Becky Skillman. It is no wonder she is the first woman elected to be Indiana's lieutenant governor and perhaps will be its next governor.

Sandy Eisenberg Sasso

A New Kind of Storyteller

*A*s a 25-year-old rabbinical student, Sandy Eisenberg Sasso strode to the podium of a New York City hotel in 1972 and criticized her faith for suppressing female perspectives. "There is an urgent need to balance the predominantly masculine perspective in Judaism with a feminine counterpart," the Philadelphia native told delegates at the American Jewish Committee's annual convention. It was a groundbreaking and gutsy speech that received coverage in the *New York Times* and other major newspapers. Sasso spoke out because she was determined to reform the religion she loves, not because she savors attention. In casual conversations outside her circle of friends and classmates, she often avoided revealing her career goal—to break into the all-male ranks of rabbis.

"Sandy gives the impression of being a quiet, even a shy, person. But there is a deeper inner strength and conviction that comes forth when she is dealing with things that are important to her," says Rabbi Dennis Sasso, her husband.

In 1974, Sandy Sasso became the second woman in the United States to be ordained as a rabbi (the first, a Cincinnati woman, had joined the rabbinate two years earlier). She and Dennis—who'd been classmates and married while in seminary—had a son two years later, making her the first rabbi to be a mother. And when the couple moved to Indianapolis's Congregation Beth-El Zedeck in 1977, they were the first husband-and-

photo: *Rich Clark*

wife team to jointly lead a congregation. The Sassos are still leading the thriving northside temple more than three decades later.

Sandy Sasso broke ground as an author, as well. When her son and daughter were young, Sasso noticed there were few books about God she wanted to read to them. The stories, she thought, were too preachy and dogmatic, and didn't invite children to use their imagination. For a class she was taking at Christian Theological Seminary in Indianapolis, Sasso wrote the kind of story she wished she could find in libraries. Called "God's Paintbrush," it invited children to encounter God through moments in their own lives.

Encouraged by her husband, Sasso sought a publisher, a trying six-year process. Many religious publishers in the 1980s only were interested in books that looked at religion in the traditional way. Secular publishers, meanwhile, weren't interested in books about religion. After twenty-three rejections, Sasso finally found a taker—a start-up in Vermont called Jewish Lights Publishing. The book debuted in 1992 and became a runaway hit. It now has more than a hundred thousand copies in print.

> Sometimes on a bright day
> when I close my eyes real tight,
> I see all kinds of colors—
> green and purple and red and blue.
> And I think these are just like God's colors.
>
> I know God's colors are in me, too.
> And I can paint with God's paintbrush.
> (from God's Paintbrush)

Since then, Sasso has written more than a dozen books, with nearly four hundred thousand copies in print. Her books are sold internationally, and have been translated into German, Italian, Spanish, and Hebrew. Many cover religious themes in a nondenominational way. Often, they raise questions men might not have thought to ask. In *Noah's Wife*, for instance, Sasso fleshed out a character who goes nameless in the Bible. Drawing on an ancient text, Sasso calls her Naamah—Hebrew for "pleasing." Before the great flood, Sasso writes, God called upon Naamah to gather the seeds of every type of plant on Earth, even the lowly dandelion, and bring them safely to the ark.

Sasso doesn't write books to persuade children to share her beliefs. "I write about a God I can believe in, in hopes that our children find a God they can believe in, too," she says.

She says the stakes are huge. "Children have more than minds and bodies. They have souls. We neglect them at our own and their peril."

Sasso hadn't set out to be a trailblazer. When she was 16, she began thinking about becoming a rabbi because she enjoyed being active in her Philadelphia synagogue and was fascinated by Jewish studies. But like most adolescents, she wanted to fit in. She told almost no one about her dream of being a rabbi, and sometimes tried to push the idea out of her mind.

"I must say I fluctuated in my decision, thinking, 'This would be the greatest thing in the world,' to thinking, 'Who do I think I am?' and 'I shouldn't even consider doing this,'" she recalls.

When Sasso enrolled at Philadelphia's Temple University in 1965, she chose English as a major. But she switched to religion in her second year. Even so, by the time she'd reached her senior year, Sasso had decided to pursue an advanced degree in religion rather than go into the seminary. She changed course again following graduation after helping with services in her home synagogue and realizing how much she enjoyed the experience. The next fall, she enrolled at Philadelphia's recently opened Reconstructionist Rabbinical College, which had decided to accept women. She was the first.

The more she studied, the larger the void she saw. In rabbinical school, "I read of men's struggles with God, but not women's. No one was answering my questions. In fact, no one was asking them," Sasso says. "I came to realize over time that my goal was not just to fit in, but to bring who I was to the rabbinate,"

Sasso scoured ancient texts to learn as much as she could about often-sketchy female biblical figures. And when one of their classmates had a daughter, Sandy and Dennis wrote a ceremony to honor her birth since baby girls didn't have a custom that carried the same sense of religious importance as the circumcision ceremony for boys. The Sassos' ceremony—and a second written by another rabbi and his wife—helped form the basis for what now is Judaic tradition, wrote Debra Nussbaum Cohen in her book *Celebrating Your New Jewish Daughter*. Since that time, Cohen writes, "welcoming the birth or adoption of baby girls has become a quiet revolution in all sectors of the Jewish community."

★ ★ ★

Sandy Eisenberg grew up in Philadelphia in a close-knit middle-class family. She said her parents "supported me in any decision I made. Even so, the idea of my becoming a rabbi must have sounded a little unusual to them."

Her father, Irv, an insurance agent, had grown up in a Jewish Orthodox household, adhering to a strict set of rules. Her mother, Freda, a homemaker and community volunteer, had been raised in a household that followed Jewish customs but rarely went to synagogue.

The Eisenbergs raised Sandy and her younger brother, Floyd, in a Reform congregation, the most liberal stream of Judaism. Sasso said she learned something about being assertive from her mother. "My mother was a very strong person. She didn't work outside the home, but she spoke her mind."

Her parents stood behind Sandy as she set out on what was sure to be a difficult career path. "They never said, 'Are you out of your mind? What could you be thinking?'" Sasso recalls. "That was helpful."

She received strong encouragement from rabbis at her synagogue, Keneseth Israel. Sasso took a Jewish history class there in high school, using a textbook that included one paragraph on women's role in Judaism. Knowing Sandy's interest in the rabbinate, the rabbi asked her to read a sentence out loud that noted there were not yet women rabbis.

"I remember reading it and putting a lot of emphasis on 'yet,'" Sasso says.

Especially influential and supportive was the synagogue's senior rabbi, Bertram Korn, a former military chaplain with a deep, booming voice. As a youth, Sasso says, "he was a very powerful figure to me. He was one of the best orators I have ever known. People came just to hear his sermon."

Sasso thought to herself, "I want to do what he does."

Korn helped her apply to rabbinical school and served as a mentor during her five years of study.

"He always had an open door," Sasso says. "He'd say, 'Tell me what your problems are, tell me what you are facing.'"

That was crucial because the community at large wasn't especially supportive. A few months into her first year, Sasso received a letter from a woman she'd never met who'd read a newspaper article about her plan to become a rabbi. The woman wrote: "I just don't know what would prompt a Jewish girl to have the 'chutzpah' to consider herself eligible to become a rabbi. . . . Ordinarily I would sign off wishing much success, but this time I will refrain. I hope you don't make it—for your sake, mine and for everyone else's."

Sasso faced other discouraging words. Just before her ordination, she spoke at a large Philadelphia synagogue about women and Judaism. After her speech, the rabbi stood up and told her, "When you grow up, you'll change your mind." (He's the one who ultimately changed his mind; he later voted in favor of ordination of women for his branch of Judaism.)

The rejection stirred a tempest of emotions.

"It actually made me want to pursue the rabbinate even more strongly," Sasso says. "But I can't say I was happy about those remarks, and there were times I wondered how in the world am I ever going to be accepted in this community if this is what's happening."

Sasso wasn't trying to be a rabble-rouser. When she spoke publicly, she made a point of striking a tone that sounded open and understanding, not angry. And early on, she always wore dresses, rather than pants, because she thought that would make the audience more receptive to her message.

While some critics couched their objections in Jewish law and tradition, she concluded that wasn't the real reason for their antagonism.

"It had a lot to do with sociological issues," she says. "There was a general discomfort in society at that time with seeing women in positions of authority."

This was the late 1960s and early 1970s, a time of upheaval for the role of women throughout society. Sasso recalled that *Ms.* magazine was one of the few places she could read what women were doing and what feminism was about. But it was an incomplete picture. It talked about women becoming doctors, lawyers, and businesspeople, but not about following the path she had chosen. "I remember buying every *Ms.* magazine that came onto the stands to hear what they had to say about women and religion. And they had nothing to say," she says.

She felt the same void in the Jewish community, which was saying little about women's equal participation in religious life.

"When I was reading scripture, biblical texts, any sacred sources of the tradition, I often asked questions men in the class never thought of asking. There were women's stories and voices that were missing. Nobody noticed that before, and it was the first thing that came to my attention.

"I had to find a path for myself which spoke to my Jewish soul and my feminist soul, and I had to find a way to bring the two together.

"Take the biblical tale of Lot and his wife. With the cities of Sodom and Gomorrah doomed to destruction because of the vile lifestyle of their inhabitants, God told Lot and his wife, 'Escape for your life! Do not look behind you nor stay anywhere in the plain. Escape to the mountains, lest you be destroyed.' As fire and brimstone fell from the sky, Lot's wife looked back toward the destruction, and she became a pillar of salt. The story is widely interpreted as one of punishment for an act of disobedience.

"This always bothered me a great deal because it meant that women were fickle and not very attentive," Sasso says.

Sasso pored through ancient rabbinic texts to research the wife, finding sources that said her name was Idit and that she turned around because her daughters were following her. The pillar of salt, she concluded, was Idit's tears. "So, it was a different way of telling the story," Sasso says. "If I were she, I would have turned around, too. You are bound to turn out of compassion for your family, and perhaps for life destroyed, no matter how terrible it was."

In a speech at a 2002 convention that celebrated women in the rabbinate, Sasso said that female rabbis were more likely to emphasize "inclusivity, a sensitivity to those on the periphery and a belief that difference doesn't mean superiority or inferiority."

She noted that studies have found women leaders are "less concerned with rank, listen more and interrupt less. Their reaction to stress is not flight or fight but tend and befriend."

Though Sasso was the only female in her eight-person seminary class, she felt none of the prejudice she endured from the broader Jewish community. One of the first students she met at seminary was Dennis Sasso, who was raised in Panama and had come to the United States to attend Brandeis University near Boston. Sandy was struck by his intelligence and sense of humor. He sometimes punned trilingually—in his native tongue of Spanish, in Hebrew, and in English. Initially, Sandy and Dennis studied together, but she was dating another student in the class. "Within a few months, I was able to break in there," Dennis quips. It was a whirlwind romance, and by February of their first year, they were engaged. They married that June.

"I just thought she was very pretty, very bright, and very much the woman I wanted to spend the rest of my life with," Dennis says.

When they returned to school on Monday after their weekend engagement, Dennis told their professor, who dismissed it as a joke and began teaching. Later in the class, he leaned over to Sandy and asked if it was true. When she said yes, he put his regular lesson plan aside and the class studied Song of Songs from the Hebrew Bible, a collection of poetry about love. Rabbi Korn, who'd been so influential in Sandy's career choice, conducted the wedding ceremony.

By the time the Sassos graduated from seminary in 1974, both had completed master's degrees in religion at Temple University, which had a partnership with the seminary, and were working on doctorates there. Dennis then spent three years leading a congregation on Long Island, while Sandy led a congregation in Manhattan.

In 1977, Dennis came to Indianapolis to interview at Beth-El Zedeck. Discussions between Dennis and synagogue leaders were going well when one remarked that because of the synagogue's growth they were considering hiring a second rabbi. Dennis mentioned Sandy, and when he made a follow-up visit she came along.

Sandy interviewed at the Indianapolis synagogue with some trepidation. She'd felt welcome at her New York City synagogue, but some of her interviews for other jobs had not gone well. She'd fielded questions like, "What would happen if you got pregnant?" and, "Would you be afraid to drive in the dark?" She figured the Midwest might be less open to women in the rabbinate than the East Coast. But while Beth-El Zedeck was part of a more conservative stream of Judaism than was her New York City synagogue, it long had been progressive about involving women. Sasso said she felt welcome at Beth-El Zedeck. Members pleased to have a female rabbi told her so. Others who might have felt differently kept their misgivings to themselves.

When the Sassos moved to Indianapolis, their son, David, was a year old. Deborah was born two years later. Sandy initially worked as a rabbi part time, but switched to full time when both children were in elementary school. Then as now, she and Dennis shared most duties, including the leading of services, preaching, teaching, and counseling.

In 1986, she wrote "God's Paintbrush" for a class at Christian Theological Seminary, where she completed her doctorate of ministry in 2000. The genesis of the idea: When daughter Deborah was 6, she returned home from a Jewish camp with a picture of a gentle-looking grandfather she had drawn. Pressed for an explanation, Deborah said she'd been asked to draw a picture of God. When she'd turned in a blank page, she'd been told she had to draw something. The old man, she said, "was all I could think of."

Sasso concluded the stories Deborah had heard about faith, God, and spirit had stifled her imagination and didn't relate to her world. "Children need a variety of images when they talk about the divine, and they just weren't out there," Sasso says. "I wanted children to be able to see God as that which gives them the strength to do something they didn't know they were able to do, which makes them aware of the special gifts they have." Sasso's tender, open-ended style was cutting-edge for the time.

> When the fizz on my favorite ice cream soda tickles my nose, it makes me laugh. Maybe it makes God laugh, too.
> What makes you cry and laugh?
> What do you think would make God cry or laugh?
>
> (from God's Paintbrush)

"Children aren't afraid of questions without answers until we make them afraid," Sasso said in a 2002 interview marking the tenth anniversary of the publication of God's Paintbrush. "Books of faith ought to be filled more with awe than answers." Sasso uses the same techniques to engage the children who attend Beth-El Zedeck. The congregation, at 600 W. 70th Street, has about 950 families as members, many of them with children.

The Sassos arrived at a difficult time in the history of the synagogue. Its beloved rabbi of the previous fifteen years, Sidney Steiman, had died the year before. "It was a relatively subdued congregation still mourning the loss," longtime member Nancy Bate wrote in a 2002 tribute honoring the Sassos' twenty-five years leading Beth-El Zedeck.

Under the couple's leadership, membership in Beth-El Zedeck has swelled, spurring construction projects that have increased the size of its building by a third. The temple also launched an early-childhood education program, which now serves more than two hundred children, and added to its adult-education offerings. In her tribute, Bate said the Sassos also enriched the congregation in less tangible ways.

"You possess an all-too-rare ability to empathize with each individual member of our large and diverse synagogue," she wrote. "You make each one of them feel as if he or she is your most important—your only—concern."

The congregation embraces the Judaic principle of Tikkun olam—the repair of the world. With the encouragement of Sandy and Dennis, members helped organize Habitat for Humanity's first all-Jewish "build." Beth-El Zedeck also has been active in myriad other causes, including the Kenya Global Interfaith Partnership, resettling Russian Jews, and helping the needy by making donations and volunteering at Gleaner's Food Bank, Julian Center, Cathedral Soup Kitchen, and Dress for Success. Sandy is co-chair of the Indianapolis Interfaith Clergy Group and a former chair of Spirit and Place, an annual citywide festival celebrating diversity, the arts, and religion. The Sassos also foster spiritual discussion in central Indiana through a monthly column they alternate writing for the *Indianapolis Star*.

But perhaps the most striking evidence of Sandy's success and influence is that she is no longer so unusual. Three of the four streams of Judaism (Reform, Conservative, and Reconstructionist, but not Orthodox) now have women rabbis, and seminary classes tend to be about half women. Hundreds of women rabbis now are leading congregations in the United States.

The publishing world also has undergone a sea change. Many authors of religious children's books have set aside the heavy-handed style that turned off Sasso when her children were young. And the bookshelves in her Beth-El Zedeck office now are filled with tomes on women and faith—the topics no one was talking or writing about when she entered the seminary.

It's a transformation women can celebrate. But Sasso's quest also was about something more personal—having the determination and conviction to pursue her calling. Sasso is glad she stood up for herself. She said working as a rabbi is filled with poignant moments. Within the span of a few days, she and Dennis might conduct a baby-naming, a bar mitzvah, a wedding, and a funeral.

"There is a jumping up and down of emotions," she says. "It gives you a certain perspective on life. It constantly calls us back to what is of ultimate significance." Such moments, she says, are reminders of the importance of hugging someone you love or picking up a phone to call a friend.

Sasso said many of her most rewarding moments as a rabbi have involved conversations with children about spirituality. Her 1994 book *In God's Name* invites children to come up with their own names for God, based on what they most value in the world. At Beth-El Zedeck, Sasso often asks children to name their God. A child whose mother was suffering from cancer answered "Healer."

"There are moments like that," she says, "when you think the things you have said, and how you've acted, have made an impact beyond what you might have imagined."

Mercy Okanemeh Obeime

The People's Champion

"My people are dying. My people are dying and I must help them," says Mercy Obeime, a respected Hoosier physician and native of the Federal of Republic Nigeria. Although she has lived in this country almost twenty years, the ties to her homeland are strong and true. She treasures her heritage and will not forget the people she left behind.

Born October 31, 1963, Obeime was baptized in St. Anthony's Catholic Church seven days later. Her given name, Okanemeh, came to her father in a dream. The literal translation in English is Immaculate, but her father prophetically chose to call her Mercy. She grew up in the rural town of Uromi, population about fifty thousand, where poverty was the accepted norm and the most fortunate had barely enough. She was the oldest of Dominic and Maria Agbonhese's ten children. The family lived in a cement block house on General Hospital Road about one mile from the downtown market. The children shared two bedrooms. There was no indoor plumbing.

About twice the size of California, Nigeria is the most populous country in Africa with an estimated population of more than 130 million. It is far from the richest, despite ample oil supplies. From the time of its independence from the United Kingdom in 1960, the country has been governed by a series of corrupt military regimes. Much of its oil

riches have been squandered to the detriment of the people whose life expectancy rate is one of the lowest in the world at less than 47 years. Poverty has led to harsh living conditions and poor access to health care.

The Agbonheses were luckier than some. Mercy's parents both were elementary school teachers. Dominic completed the coursework necessary to obtain a locally issued teaching certificate, and then waited until Mercy was 16 to move to England for two years to earn a bachelor of arts degree from the University of Bristol. He returned to accept the position of vice principal at Agba Grammar School. Maria carried the load at home during his absence.

Perhaps benefiting from being the first child of two educators who spent quality time with their daughter, Mercy was identified as a gifted child when she was barely able to walk. She and her siblings were freed from afternoon chores—tasks such as fetching water, scrubbing dishes, and washing diapers—as long as they spent the time studying. Mercy studied every afternoon.

At the local Catholic girls' school, she often was first in her class. It was clear she needed a bigger challenge. At 11, Mercy was sent to Federal Government Girls College, a boarding school for talented girls of elementary and high school age in Benin City, about an hour's drive from Uromi. Mercy's parents could not afford to pay for any of her school-related expenses, but fortunately the school was operated by the government, which provided tuition and room and board for all of its students.

Boarding school was a frightening and stressful experience for a young girl who had never left home. When Mercy arrived, for example, she learned that Uromi, which she thought was the center of the earth, was not even on the state map at her school. Many of her classmates had come from larger cities and even other countries. No one was from her hometown. She wondered if she had come from a place that did not exist.

At school, students shared their ambitions and goals with counselors. Mercy was not aware of the broad range of possibilities that lay before her until she learned at school that medicine, accounting, engineering, and other such professions were within her grasp. She realized that she could be anything she wanted to be. Mercy was proficient in sciences, but languages caused her difficulty. English was the official language of Nigeria but in her village Mercy spoke the native Ishan much of the time. She persevered and succeeded brilliantly.

During her fifth year, Mercy was serving on the school's selection committee when physician John Oriaifo moved his family to Uromi—to a house across the street from her family's—and his daughter Ejemeh applied for admission. Mercy was excited when she noticed an Ishan name and an address that was almost identical to her own; in her time there, no one else from her town had attended the school. She met Ejemeh and her parents and an instant friendship was forged. During visits home, Mercy took every opportunity to shadow Dr. Oriaifo, who had trained in London in obstetrics and gynecology, and began to consider a career in medicine. Ejemeh enrolled in the school and is now a practicing pediatrician at Johns Hopkins University. They remain friends.

The Nigerian education system is comprised of a five-year high school program followed by an optional curriculum called A-levels, consisting of two years of higher education. A-Levels act as a bridge between high school and medical school, which takes an additional six years. Mercy enrolled in the A-levels program and took courses in physics, biology, and chemistry.

She also worked every summer. In high school, she taught mathematics to students preparing for high school graduation exams. During the summer of her A-levels, she worked with Dr. Oriaifo in the hospital, first as a receptionist in registration. Later, she rotated within the hospital, often working in the pharmacy or research department. The summer before medical school, she worked with Dr. Oriaifo as an operating room assistant. Afterward she washed the instruments, a dangerous job because they were covered with blood and tissue. She was unaware of the necessity to wear gloves. She was lucky.

Due in large part to the influence of Dr. Oriaifo, Mercy enrolled in medical school at the University of Benin, located within walking distance of her high school. She wanted to be a physician specializing in Ob-Gyn just like her mentor. The state continued to pay all expenses.

Mercy was still in medical school in 1987, when she met another doctor in another life-changing encounter. Chris Obeime, who had emigrated from Uromi to the United States at age 20 to attend college, was back visiting his parents for Christmas. He had graduated from Indiana University as an optometrist in 1981 (later, he became a dermatologist), and his cousin Patrick Egbase, a physician at Mercy's school, told Chris "she would be a perfect wife." When Chris saw Mercy on the street of their hometown, he was smitten and asked his brother to make an introduction. In Nigeria, marriages are arranged to some degree and introductions are generally brokered in this manner. When they met on Christmas Day 1987, Chris had little time for romance; he had to return to the United States on January 2. He asked Mercy to lunch on December 29. She accepted and brought all of her siblings. A frustrated Chris left before the couple could really get to know one another. He was discouraged, but they agreed to stay in touch. Through an increasingly warm correspondence, Mercy finally was convinced to visit him in Indianapolis in October 1988. By December of that year, Chris was back in Nigeria pursuing her. Mercy visited again the following April, and on August 5, 1989, Mercy Agbonhese became Mercy Obeime and settled in Indianapolis.

That first Hoosier winter caused her to second-guess her decision. In Nigeria, about two hundred miles north of the equator, temperatures range from 70 degrees to 110 degrees. There is no autumn, winter, or spring. Mercy Obeime had no idea what they were. She had never seen snow. Shortly after she arrived, she experienced a blizzard. It scared her to the point that she was ready to hibernate between October and April. Today, she loves Indianapolis and its four seasons.

The transition from the University of Benin to practicing in the United States was challenging. Medical training in Nigeria is not as hands-on as it is in America. Obeime's education was literally by the book. Even that was difficult. While studying, Obeime read that a certain cancer of the uterus looked like a bunch of grapes. She had never seen grapes. There was no internet at the time, so she just had to set that concept aside until she determined what grapes looked like. Practical training would come later.

In 1990, while studying in the medical school library for the required Foreign Graduate Certificate exams, Obeime met Dr. Joseph Christian, who led the Department of Genetics at Indiana University. He had noticed her studying every day and struck up a conversation. When Christian learned of her desire to practice medicine in the United States, he granted Obeime a two-year fellowship taking care of children with congenital abnormalities.

Because of her relationship with Dr. Christian, Obeime became excited about the field of genetics and wanted to make it part of her practice. But she was not interested in the prenatal aspects an Ob-Gyn would specialize in; rather, she wanted to focus on age-onset conditions such as Huntington's disease and Alzheimer's. So Obeime gave up the dream of starting an Ob-Gyn practice and chose to specialize in family medicine, reasoning that she still could deliver babies in addition to other duties. It did not turn out that way—she hasn't delivered a baby since 1996.

After passing the Foreign Graduate Certificate exams, Obeime did a family practice residency at Indiana University from 1993 to 1996. She became friends with her surgical rotation mentor, Dr. Paul Strange. As they worked together, Dr. Strange persuaded Obeime to interview with the hospital where he held privileges, St. Francis on the south side of Indianapolis. During this process, St. Francis personnel were reluctant to recommend the family practice clinic located in an economically disadvantaged neighborhood near Southern and Madison avenues, for fear of losing the bright young recruit. "You don't want to practice medicine here," they told her. "These patients don't have a lot of money, and they are older and more difficult." Obeime was undeterred. "This is where I want to practice. I have seen poverty before."

Obeime was appointed medical director of the St. Francis Neighborhood Health Center in 1996 and still serves in that capacity twelve years later. She has made the clinic a special place. Its mission is to provide primary and preventive care to families who cannot afford health insurance. Patients are charged only what they can pay without compromising their financial integrity. Oftentimes the patients have no food or housing; the clinic staff—which includes social workers, nutritionists, and a pregnancy coordinator—takes care of both. There also is a commissary where baby clothing, diapers, and strollers can be obtained. The clinic loses money and is underwritten by St. Francis.

In 2001 at the age of 38, tall and slender and looking more like a movie star than a physician, Obeime was enjoying a fulfilling career in family practice, tending to a patient population that needed her. She was married with three children—daughters Ivie and Jeme and son Jalu—and was largely content. Then a traumatic experience changed her life forever.

As a favor to a friend, Obeime visited Nigeria during a vacation to recruit pharmacists for CVS Pharmacy. She was successful, finding forty-four pharmacists for CVS and three for St. Francis. Obeime was euphoric because she knew she had positively affected the lives of fellow Nigerians. In that state of mind, she dropped by her hometown of Uromi to say hello to her family, with whom she continues to maintain a close relationship despite their distance. On the way, she decided to visit one of her medical school professors, Dr. Egie Ukpommwan, who had recently opened a clinic. Dressed in jeans and a shirt, she arrived at the doctor's office only to learn from the nurse that he was away at a meeting. The nurse was unfriendly to Obeime, who looked very much like the native population. When Obeime asked to use the office telephone to call the doctor, the nurse said it would cost money. Obeime was incredulous, but nonetheless beckoned to her brother, who had some Nigerian nairas.

While waiting for her brother to come in from the car, she noticed that the nurse was trying to prevent a man from carrying a woman into an examining room. "You have to stop here first," the nurse screamed, sensing a loss of control. It was obvious to Obeime that the man did not have the necessary 250 nairas (about $2) to register the patient. She assured the nurse that she would pay the fee as soon as her brother arrived with the money, but was told they would have to wait until the bill was paid in full.

While they argued, the man made his way into the exam room. Obeime decided to investigate. "I am a doctor. I will look at her," she told him, although she was terrified. Because of the AIDS epidemic, she had been warned not to have close contact with sick patients in Nigeria, especially without protective gloves. She asked the nurse for gloves but was refused. The patient began to gasp. Obeime asked the nurse for oxygen but again was refused. She went back to the woman and watched her die. The man said his wife had been sick and getting worse. He had taken her to a clinic, where she got a cursory examination and he was given a list, which Obeime read. It included supplies for IV fluid (for dehydration), vitamin B complex, Amoxicillin (which is used to treat bacterial infections), tetracycline (a broad-spectrum antibiotic), and some pain medicine. The clinic had prescribed just about everything to see what might work, but the man did not have money to buy any of the supplies. He had heard that the new clinic might help, so he picked up his wife and brought her over, only to find that the doctor was not in.

For the first time, Obeime noticed a boy of 5 or 6 holding onto the woman's clothes, wailing. "Mama, Mama, I've been telling you I am hungry all day. You didn't get up to get me food. I'm hungry, I'm dying of hunger." Obeime broke down, crying. Her son was about the same age and his biggest concern that morning when she called home had been whether his homework should go into a blue folder or a red folder. This Nigerian boy was struggling with abject hunger, the fatal loss of his mother, and a father who had no money.

The clinic was chaotic. Not wanting to be charged for the clinic visit, the man snatched up his dead wife and began to sneak out of the room. Obeime asked him to put her back on the cot, assuring him that he would not be charged. The man began to scream, cursing God, "You have betrayed me. I have asked you to help me and I believed you are going to help me but look what I have ended up with. I have no idea what to do with my wife's body, I have no idea what to do with my son."

God did not need to come from heaven and save this woman, Obeime thought. Intravenous fluids alone might have been enough. When Obeime's brother came in with the money, she gave much of it to the man and asked him to feed his son. Finally, the doctor returned. "Mercy, why are you crying?" he asked. When she explained, he still did not understand. "Why is this your problem? You came from America to see me, why are you worrying about some man whose wife died? Why are you worrying about this man and his dead wife? Just forget about that."

But it was all Obeime could think about.

"Right now that's the only thing that's important because that woman was somebody," she told her professor. "I couldn't do anything, in spite of everything I learned in medical school. Nothing was happening." At that moment, she made up her mind to help change the situation. The problem, Obeime thought, was supplies. "Okay," she said to no one in particular, "I will start sending supplies. My people are dying. My people are dying and I must help them." For two years, she collected medicine and sent it over with whoever was visiting Nigeria. But it never seemed to be enough. Obeime wanted to make a larger impact.

In May 2003, at the recommendation of Senator Richard Lugar, the Reverend Kent Millard of St. Luke's United Methodist Church helped Obeime organize the Mercy Foundation to raise money to purchase drugs and medical supplies for Nigeria. Later, the Mercy Foundation took on other initiatives, including one to help obese patients in Indianapolis. Its mission is to restore hope. "If we let people devalue another's life, like the woman in the clinic, if she is treated like a fly on the water, without further thought, what would prevent a terrorist from coming to Nigeria and convincing people who believe they have no worth to become suicide bombers, blow up New York, and kill a million people?" Obeime asks.

All Obeime requested for her 40th birthday in 2003 was to be able to go to Nigeria to deliver a mass of supplies—enough to really make a difference. In January 2004, she and her husband and his cousin Andrew Oghina personally took valuable medical supplies to Nigeria. Obeime bought them at a huge discount from the American Academy of Family Physicians, which has a foundation that sends an airplane full of supplies to medical missions in Russia, Uzbekistan, and other places. Obeime purchased the leftovers, distributing the supplies to doctors in Uromi, including her neighbor, Dr. Oriaifo. It made a difference, but it was not enough. Obeime arranged for a second mission, then encountered a problem no one had contemplated.

Before embarking on the second mission, Obeime communicated with the Nigerian minister of health. He had visited Indiana and met the Obeimes two months before. He enthusiastically supported the mission trip, but when the supplies arrived at Murtala Muhammed Airport in Nigeria, officials imposed a $14,000 tax. Obeime did not have $14,000—she had not even paid that much for the supplies—so the shipment was confiscated and never returned. She tried everything to get the cargo back, including communication with the president of Nigeria. According to Obeime, high-ranking officials in government were involved. She was devastated.

Six months later, after talking to everyone she could—including the chairman of the ruling party, who was from Uromi—she finally received the boxes back. They were empty. The medicine had disappeared. Obeime had no idea what to do until a chance meeting later that year with a Johns Hopkins physician who had been traveling to Nigeria with drugs. How did he do it? "Simple," he said. "I smuggled them. They don't come in boxes, they come in my suitcases with my personal belongings. Lots of suitcases, lots of medicine." Obeime followed her colleague's advice and defied the corrupt public officials.

Obeime has been recognized throughout her career for her work with the less fortunate. She was chosen as the national winner of the 2003 Spirit of Women Award in the health care provider category for her work at St. Francis. This award was created by an association of hospitals across the country to celebrate women who accomplish extraordinary deeds. As a result of the award, she was a guest on NBC's *Today Show*. In 2004, she was chosen as a Local Legend after a nomination by U.S. congresswoman Julia Carson. The Local Legend award is sponsored by the National Library of Medicine in Bethesda, Maryland, and celebrates the contribution of female physicians to the health of their communities and our country.

Obeime continues to organize trips to Uromi. If she has involved others in her dangerous-but-vital smuggling operation, she will not say. She just wants to make a difference. "When people come to me totally helpless and I am able to do something that actually puts a smile on their faces and makes them feel like they are treated like human beings, then I feel like it was worth my day to have gone to work. I have done something that day." One cannot measure the number of lives Mercy Okanemeh Obeime has influenced, perhaps saved. This people's champion has bettered our world.

Jeanette Lee

The Black Widow

Late one spring afternoon in New York City in 1989, a 17-year-old girl on her way home from waitressing decided on a lark to walk into Chelsea Billiards, the new pool hall on 21st Street, after hearing her friends discussing the movie *The Color of Money*. She heard the click-clack of pool balls from the back of the room. The girl, a tall, slender, attractive, Korean American, had never witnessed a game of pool. She was fascinated. She watched while a man, cue in hand, bent over the table and pocketed one ball after another. His movements were graceful, as if in a ballet. She could almost hear the rhythm of his heartbeat. She could feel his breathing. She gaped at the scene—the colors, the angles, the symmetry, the beauty, the sounds—and left the pool hall many hours later having made a life-altering decision. The young girl ached to learn the game of pool, but more than that she wanted to excel. Five years later, Jeanette Lee, known as the Black Widow, was ranked as the best female player in the world.

Lee's parents, Sonja and John Tak, were born in Korea and immigrated to New York after the Korean War. Eventually, all seven of her mother's siblings and her parents and grandparents joined them in New York City, living in the same co-op building in Brooklyn's lower-middle-class Crown Heights neighborhood. In 1976, when Jeanette was 5, her parents divorced. Both remarried. In addition to a blended family of two step-

brothers and two half-sisters, Jeanette has one natural sister, Doris, who is older and lives in Hong Kong with her husband and two children. Doris has a master's degree in International Studies from Columbia University and speaks nine languages, including both dialects of Chinese. Their step-father, Bo Chun Lee, whom Lee calls Dad, adopted the girls. He owns a smoke shop in New York City selling cigarettes, magazines, candy, and lottery tickets. Her mother, Sonja Lee, is a registered nurse.

At age 12, Lee was diagnosed with scoliosis, a curvature of the spine. On an X-ray, her spine looks more like an "S" than a straight line. She underwent a number of operations, well into adulthood, including a fol-low-up operation when a spinal fusion was not successful. Her doctors had to remove scar tissue and re-fuse the vertebrae. At the same time they inserted rods. When her body rejected some of the hardware, they had to go back and remove it. Because of the many operations, her spine now is completely fused, limiting her mobility. She can bend over, but she can-not rotate except through her ankles. Lee is in constant pain. Still, she has not let it slow her down. "I could sit here and rot on the couch and be depressed or I can just decide how I want to spend this life the way God made me," she says.

As a teenager, Lee tested into the prestigious Bronx Science High School, a school specializing in math and science for gifted children. She pictured herself as a thinner, less pretty version of her sister Doris. She wore glasses and lived in a neighborhood where her ethnicity was de-meaned. Lee had vague aspirations to be an artist or an actress or a teacher, but lacking confidence and not sure what she wanted to do, she dropped out of school at age 16. She passed the Graduate Equivalency Diploma examination and went to work waiting tables for a short time before fol-lowing a high school sweetheart to the University of Buffalo, eventually enrolling there. When the romance cooled, the 17-year-old returned to New York City to work and study early childhood development at Queens Community College. Lee's mother counseled her on the impor-tance of academic achievement, and she changed her major to elementary education before losing interest in her coursework.

From the moment Lee wandered into Chelsea Billiards, she spent all of her free time practicing pool—against her doctor's orders. It was all she could think about. While riding the subway, she would hold her hand up and try to angle her wrist to stay under her elbow so that it swung perfectly. Even in her dreams she imagined balls glancing off other balls. Everything was an angle—geometry in real time. Pool is in large part a mental game, and Lee's math acuity and ability to concentrate perfectly matched these challenges. "The difference between winning and losing is all in your mind," Lee says. As her pool skills began to improve, she dropped out of college and devoted herself to pool, thinking that if that failed she could always go back to school. She hung out at Chelsea Billiards between shifts at the restaurant. She practiced night and day. Her mother was not happy.

Lee worked part-time at Howard Beach Billiards Club, one of her favorite billiards parlors. After closing one night in 1991, owner Gabe Vigorito reminisced with Lee about the first time he had seen her in the club. The club had not been open long. She had walked in, dressed—as usual—in black. Despite her choice of clothing, she looked sweet and alluring, soft and safe. But with the first rack of balls, her demeanor changed. When she leaned into her stance, her long black hair lay across her back and her eyes shone with the same intensity as a leopard's during the first moments of chase. One by one, the balls careened against the rails and into the pockets. Vigorito said she had reminded him of a black widow—a spider that comes out at night, draws in its victims, and then eats them alive. The moniker stuck. Although Lee was bothered at first when people referred to her as the Black Widow, today she embraces the name. "It's actually a bit liberating. It allows me to be a little spunky," she says.

Shortly thereafter, when Vigorito celebrated his grand opening, he set up a match featuring Lee and Willie Mosconi, who was known as Mr. Pocket Billiards and considered to be one of the best players in the history of the game. It was a thrill for Lee because it was her first opportunity to showcase her expertise in front of a significant crowd. Vigorito became

Lee's mentor and helped her to market the Black Widow persona while promoting his club. He prepared tri-fold brochures challenging players to "Break balls with the Black Widow."

By age 20, Lee was the best player in New York City but had yet to compete in international tournaments. That year she came in second in a state championship but despite that made it to the Women's Professional Billiards Association national championship in Milwaukee, Wisconsin, because the winner was unable to attend. Vigorito gave her $500 to go clothes shopping on the condition that the outfits she purchased were all black.

Lee had never ventured out of the state of New York, let alone to a national tournament. In December 1991, she walked into the arena and saw many, many players—competent players—all older. She had never seen an assemblage like this before. The tournament was match play with double elimination. The game was "9-ball." It seems simple: The winner is the first player to pocket the nine ball. But it's not quite that easy. On every shot, the cue ball must first contact the lowest numbered ball on the table. A player continues to shoot until failing to pocket a ball. An overwhelmed Lee came in tied for 17th, with two wins and two losses. That would be her worst finish ever.

Lee entered a second national tournament the following July, the Willard's International 9-Ball Classic held in St. Charles, Illinois, about an hour west of Chicago. She came in third and received a prize of $3,500, an enormous amount of money to Lee. She calculated that she had enough money for three more tournaments. "Now when I think about it, for 96 women in the tournament I should have won more than $3,500, but at the time it was like I was rich." After that finish she was rated 28th in the nation.

In 1993, Lee won the year's first two tournaments on her way to five in all. By the end of the year, she was rated among the top ten players by *Billiards Digest*, the major billiards publication. Lee practiced incessantly. "I really had the frame of mind that the only way I'm going to be the best in the world is if I am more committed, mind and body, than everyone else in the world. That means you need to be playing when everyone else is partying, sleeping in, or going to movies. If you are working hard at your game, you're going to be tough to beat," she says. By October 1994, she was the No. 1 ranked player in the world by the Women's Professional Billiards Association (WPBA) and received the "Player of the Year Award" from *Billiards Digest*. It was perhaps the sharpest rise from obscurity of anyone in the game.

Sonja Lee, who had wanted her daughter to stay in school and pursue a career befitting her extraordinary intellect, was never really pleased with her choice to play pool for a living, although she did try to be supportive. After Lee earned Player of the Year honors, Sonja presented her with a gold bangle bracelet and earrings that looked like an Olympic wreath. It was the first time that she had acknowledged Lee's accomplishments and said, "I am proud of you." It was a monumental moment.

Leveraging her celebrity status, Lee secured the position of national spokesperson for the Bicycle Club Casino in Los Angeles. This enabled her to supplement her tournament winnings with a steady, reliable income. She moved to L.A. in 1995. Later that year, she had another life-changing experience. During a national tournament at the Bicycle Club, she met fellow contestant—and native Hoosier—George Breedlove, who was ranked sixth in the world. Lee never thought she would marry someone in the business, but it was one of those encounters where everything went just right. Breedlove proposed on the third date and Lee said yes right away. Two weeks later, Breedlove flew to New York to formally ask Lee's parents for her hand in marriage—which they denied until he eventually won them over. "He was everything I didn't know I needed," Lee says. They were married on January 6, 1996.

Lee's new husband moved from Indianapolis to join her in California, where the newlyweds lived for about two years. Breedlove has two daughters from a prior marriage and although he and his daughters often exchanged visits, it wasn't enough for him. Lee remembered her childhood and the trauma of separation from her biological father, whom she did not see for more than twenty years after her parents' divorce. She understood what Breedlove's daughters must have been experiencing and suggested to him that they move to Indiana. "I told him, 'I travel for a living. I will be fine,' and that's what we did. We moved closer to Morgan and Olivia. And now I am a Hoosier through and through," Lee says. Breedlove has since retired from the pro tour in order to pursue business interests in Indiana.

Family remains very important to both of them, despite their difficulties having biological children together. After a miscarriage, they adopted a daughter, Cheyenne, in 2004 as an infant and, because she travels with her mother, she has seen the world. In 2007, they became legal guardians of a 14-year-old boy, John Kang, who was in foster care and needed a permanent home. They knew right away that they had to take him in.

Lee's childhood dreams of being an artist, actress, or teacher seemed all but impossible, but today she is all three. Lee loves to paint, although she rarely has time. She would like to try sculpting. And, of course, there is artistry in her sport. Lee also is an actress, having appeared as herself in a number of episodes of HBO's *Arli$$*. In one episode, when the Rita character is hustled by a pool shark, she enlists the help of her cousin—the Black Widow—to exact revenge. Lee also played herself in a full-length motion picture, *The Other Sister*, a 1999 Walt Disney movie directed by Garry Marshall and starring Diane Keaton.

As her career has progressed, Lee also has become a teacher, and enjoys being a mentor to other pool players. She loves to share. She made an instructional DVD called *Black Widow Billiards* and created a teaching course titled The Black Widow Experience, both of which demonstrate not just how to hit a ball but also offer instruction on strategy, position play, pattern play, mechanics, the mental game, and trick shots. The Black Widow Experience was offered in Las Vegas at a cost of $3,000. The students were videotaped and everything about their game was evaluated and improved by instructors. At the end of the three-day course, students took on Lee individually. The Black Widow Experience was an enjoyable undertaking for Lee—but not profitable. She would like to reprise the program at a reduced price, in the hopes of attracting more customers, perhaps at a billiards club in Indiana.

Lee has also taken instruction herself. She is very analytical and considers herself self-taught, but later in her career she had mentors who helped her with strategic maneuvering and shot selection—a skill referred to in the trade as reading the green. Her most significant mentor was a dear friend, Eugene Nagy, a professional with whom she played almost every day while in her early 20s.

Lee advises young women that since life goes by so fast, it is very important to learn about yourself, who you are, your identity. If you don't know what you want to do, go out and try everything. Don't sit in your room listening to your iPod, watching TV, and listening to other people live their lives. Go out and experiment until you find out what's right for you and then give it all the passion you have. Don't be afraid of hard work.

Although she continues to play in tournaments and win prizes, Lee's star status allows her to derive most of her income through endorsements and public appearances. She is in demand for major corporate events, visiting universities and Fortune 500 companies to speak and demonstrate her skills. A typical appearance begins with a ten- to fifteen-minute address followed by a trick-shot exhibition. She often gives a fifteen-minute instructional demonstration and almost always accepts challenges from the audience. After vanquishing all comers, she poses for pictures and signs autographs on cue balls and photographs. She also has made appearances at celebrity fundraisers sponsored by the likes of NFL quarterback Reggie Bush and NBA star Shaquille O'Neal.

In 2001, just after three consecutive surgeries on her neck, back, and shoulder, Lee was selected as one of two U.S. representatives to play in the first-ever world games recognized by the International Olympic Committee. Although the sport is not played during the summer or winter Olympic Games, it is played for Olympic medals. "It was almost like a nightmare," Lee says. "I thought, are you kidding me? I've been waiting my whole life to compete for an Olympic medal and now with the games a little more than three months away I can barely get out of bed, let alone practice." Even so, Lee went on to win the gold medal, outshining sixty-three other women at the games in Akita, Japan. She considers this one of the greatest accomplishments and proudest moments of her career. Sadly, the timing of a subsequent operation prevented her from defending her Olympic championship in 2005.

Lee became the Women's World Trick Shot Challenge Champion in 2004 at the Mohegan Sun Casino in Hartford, Connecticut. She also presented a televised trick shot exhibition on *The Late Show with David Letterman* in September 2002.

In 2008, she had her last surgery, making ten surgeries in all—seven of them during her pro career. Extraordinarily enough, she has been able to come back from each surgery and maintain her ranking among the world's top five women players. In 2006, she won the World Championship in Korea, and in 2007 she won the Empress Cup competition there. According to the Empress Cup promoters, the event pitted six of the world's most talented female players against each other.

Lee continues to practice for hours at a time in a specially constructed room next to her Mooresville, Indiana, home. She owns two of the best tables in the world. One is a nine-foot pocket billiard table manufactured by Diamond Billiard Products Inc., and the other is a ten-foot carom billiard table—which has no pockets—manufactured by Gabriels, a company founded by world champion billiards player René Gabriels. Both are made with slate, like all tournament tables. The carom table is used primarily for a game called 3-Cushion Billiards, which is played with three balls. The object of the game is to make the cue ball contact the other two balls on the table and three or more rails. But the cue ball must touch a minimum of three rails before it touches the second object ball. When that occurs, a point is scored. Play generally continues until a predetermined total is reached. Lee doesn't play 3-Cushion Billiards professionally, but she enjoys playing the game and is often invited to national tournaments for which players normally would have to qualify.

On the walls of her poolroom, she displays many awards and pictures of billiards experts and other sports heroes, along with celebrities she has met at various appearances. Her Olympic medal occupies a special place in the room.

Today, Lee is a confident woman who long ago overcame her poor self-image. Although scoliosis and the myriad operations have left her in constant pain with degenerative disc disease and arthritis, she continues to work out every day and watches carefully what she eats. She sets her bar high and advises others to do the same.

Lee thinks it is important to give back to her community. She feels it is especially important for her as a role model and an ambassador to the sport. She likes what it does for her—the enhanced compassion for people has helped her develop as a human being.

After surgeries and tournament losses, she has thought about quitting the game. Even the slightest failure hurts someone who has to work so hard to be great, who has to give all of herself and make an unparalleled level of sacrifice. All that hard work should pay off. And when it doesn't, it takes strength to keep trying. "You know if you practice the same shot two thousand times in a row, that one shot, you would think you had practiced enough that it would go in every time," she says. "But it happens and you have to be able to deal with that humanness in yourself and pick yourself up off the floor and say, 'I love this enough to go through this.' It's like a child, a baby that you love, you've got to clean his diapers as much as you can go goo-goo and gaga and play with him. There are bad times that go with the good times, but it's worth it." So when she thinks about quitting she always says, "I'm not quitting, I'm going forward."

★ ★ ★

Lee's story begins with a teenage girl walking into a pool hall—but she was no ordinary teenage girl. Then and now, Jeanette Lee is extraordinarily talented and driven to be successful. She overcame physical challenges that would have left most people with a lifetime of disability to become the best billiards player in the world. This particular black widow, although ruthless at the table, is a wholesome, family-oriented role model, not just in the game of pocket billiards, but in the game of life.

Patricia R. Miller

☆

It's in the Bag

During the two years Mitch Daniels spent on the campaign trail as he sought to become governor of Indiana, he made it clear that, once elected, boosting Indiana's economic development efforts would be his top priority. Indeed, the first piece of legislation Daniels signed after taking office in 2005 created the Indiana Economic Development Corporation, the entity charged with directing the state's efforts to attract businesses to Indiana—and keep them there. Success would depend in large part upon who led the endeavor, however, and Daniels wasted no time in finding the best candidate to serve as Indiana's first secretary of commerce. Even before he was elected, he recruited a certain Fort Wayne woman to fill the post, someone he described as "one of the greatest business success stories in our state"—Patricia R. Miller.

Pat Miller and business partner Barbara Baekgaard had founded a women's handbag and accessory company, Vera Bradley Designs, in 1982 with a small bankroll and a big vision. Twenty-five years later, the fashion powerhouse had more than six hundred employees and worldwide sales in excess of $100 million. The trail to such triumph was an achievement-packed odyssey for this mother of three. Miller's success, in many ways, is astonishing—even to her.

Still, Pat (née Polito) Miller's entrepreneurial bloodlines were unmistakable to anyone familiar with her family's history. After emigrating from the

verdant hills of Termini Imerese, near Palermo, Sicily, Pat's grandfather, Santo Polito, established a grocery store to serve families drawn to Farmington, Illinois, by the booming strip-mining industry and Caterpillar plant in nearby Peoria. Three of Santo's eight children, Pat's father, Eugene, and her uncles Pete and Tony, developed a steely work ethic forged behind the family grocery counter. From the time she could barely see across that counter, Pat also was enmeshed in the family enterprise.

She learned about the world beyond Farmington from the tobacco and candy salesmen who regularly called upon the store, armed with product samples and exotic stories. Although she thought Farmington a wonderful place to grow up, Pat was convinced that she was destined for a future beyond the town limits. Neither of her parents had attended college, yet Pat knew that she surely would. In due time, she fulfilled her teenage dream of attending a "Big Ten school far from home" by enrolling at Indiana University in Bloomington, Indiana—only one state but a world apart from Farmington. Upon graduation, her life path followed a standard course consisting of career, marriage, and children, which eventually led her to Fort Wayne.

Miller had foregone her high school teaching career shortly after moving to the northeast Indiana city, where her husband, Mike, had accepted a position with a local law firm. Miller devoted herself to raising her three young boys with a smattering of volunteer work thrown in. During July and August, she made it a point to finish the household chores by 10 AM so she could devote the rest of the day to nonstop rounds of swim meets, softball games, and other of her sons' summertime activities.

Co-founding a global enterprise was the last thing on Miller's mind during the summer of 1974 as she drove her station wagon along the suburban side streets of Fort Wayne's Wildwood Park subdivision. She was en route to knock on the door of the neighborhood's newest arrival, fulfilling her volunteer role as the Wildwood Welcoming Committee—a committee of one.

Miller had her 5-year-old, Jay, along when she pulled into the new neighbor's driveway to deliver her well-practiced "Welcome to the

Neighborhood" message. She rang the doorbell and a moment or two later a slender, red-haired woman, dressed in jeans, came to the door looking as though she had just been interrupted. Miller smiled valiantly, extending one hand as she clutched young Jay in the other. The redhead sized her up and down with a rapid once over.

"Do you know how to hang wallpaper?" Barb Baekgaard asked before her visitor could utter a single word.

"Uh . . . no," Miller stammered.

"Well, c'mon in here. You're going to learn," Baekgaard responded with an inviting smile. Miller parked Jay at the kitchen table and picked up a paste brush as a new friendship—and fledgling business venture—was born. The women meshed well. Baekgaard was good at telling jokes and Miller was good at laughing at them. Before long, Miller had perfected her technique to the point that the two moms were able to launch a paper-hanging business, allowing them to enjoy flexible hours and work close to home. When it came time to name their new venture, they whimsically selected "Up Your Wall!" The duo encountered a warm reception from their fellow suburban homemakers. With Miller covering the straight walls and Baekgaard hanging around the doors and windows, they formed a business bond held tight with hard work and wallpaper paste.

Miller loaded up her basement with discontinued paper rolls she picked up regularly in Chicago for pennies apiece. Friends and neighbors loved to browse the inventory and would very often hire the women to hang whatever patterns they had selected. This "paper chase" led the pair to modest financial success, but after eight years both had grown weary of constantly washing paste from their hair. They began to cast about for less gritty opportunities, and found inspiration in 1982 during a visit with Baekgaard's parents in Florida. Baekgaard's mother directed the partners to a Palm Beach boutique, Pierre Deux, where both were impressed by the shop's quaint lines of "French Country" products, such as fabrics, rugs, lampshades, handbags, and, yes, wallpaper.

On the way back to Indiana, awaiting their connecting flight in the Atlanta airport, the women discussed their visit to Pierre Deux. They were struck with the same notion: If those fancy French fabric bags could be produced using domestic material, they would appeal to a much broader market. Their concept had its roots in history: The patterned fabrics associated with the French provincial style actually had originated in India, but high European import taxes on Indian paisleys and foulard fabrics in the nineteenth century ultimately led to their being produced in France for less. What Baekgaard and Miller had in mind would be an extension of this time-honored tradition of one culture "borrowing" from another. Excited, the women batted the idea back and forth, expanding their then-imaginary line of products to include bigger bags like duffels and shopping totes. They could sell them wholesale to women's stores, they reasoned. But not without first conducting a practice run.

In addition to their wallpaper venture, the partners were supplementing their income selling Dunn Worthington women's clothing to friends and neighbors through periodic trunk shows at their homes. Seamstress Mary Abella, one of their trusted friends and a highly capable professional, handled any onsite alterations during the shows. Upon their return from Florida, Miller and Baekgaard enlisted Abella's help to put their concept of affordable, cloth handbags—fashioned from domestic fabrics—to the test. The market test. Miller and Baekgaard each put up $250 to purchase the raw materials, visiting a local fabric store to select bolts that most resembled French provincial patterns. Delivering the material to Abella, they described the simple-yet-elegant designs inspired by the Pierre Deux bags they had admired in Florida.

The women who gathered at Baekgaard's home to view the Dunn Worthington fashions on St. Patrick's Day were greeted by a display of tasteful "country" cloth handbags, duffle bags, and sport bags. They were not informed that the bags were the creation of their hostesses, and were left to assume that they were part of the standard inventory. Miller and Baekgaard were afraid that if their friends knew who had made the bags, the women might buy them "just to be nice." Looking for a brand with which to label their new line of French Country bags, the partners adopted the name of the person who had drawn them to Florida and their inspiration: Baekgaard's mother, Vera Bradley.

When, at the end of the show, all twelve of the Vera Bradley bags had been sold, Miller and Baekgaard were convinced that they'd found a market for their dream product. And so, through the inspired efforts of two under-capitalized and over-achieving Hoosiers, Vera Bradley Designs was born. The partners soon were knocking on the doors of local area clothing buyers. First one and then a handful of buyers were convinced to gamble on the unusual line of homegrown, hand-stitched bags. Those bets paid off as customers embraced the fashionable, yet affordable, accessory that bore a "Made in the USA" label.

Before long, Miller and Baekgaard decided to bury the paste brush and devote their full-time energies to Vera Bradley Designs. One of the first to recognize the potential of the new venture was Miller's husband, who encouraged his wife and provided the fledgling company with needed legal counsel. Pat's determined "can-do" attitude was one of the attributes Mike found most attractive about his future wife when the couple met amid the ivy-covered limestone halls of Indiana University in 1960.

Although the 1952 movie starring Spencer Tracey and Katharine Hepburn was pretty much forgotten by then, the "Pat and Mike" tag still held some charm when they began dating during their senior year. Upon graduation with a freshly minted business degree in hand, Pat accepted a $6,400-per-year teaching job in Hammond, Indiana, situated in the heart of the state's fire-tempered steel-producing district known affectionately as "Da Region." Not coincidentally, Hammond also was close to Mike's hometown of Cedar Lake. Pat taught typing, shorthand, and other business skills to the children of immigrant steel workers. On weekends, she and Mike sought romantic getaway spots among the Lake Michigan sand dunes.

Pat and Mike wed in 1961. Mike enrolled at the local Indiana University law school and Pat found work as a high school teacher. Two years later, the young couple landed back in Bloomington, where Mike completed his law studies while Pat carried on in her role as a PHT (Putting Husband Through) wife. She repeatedly was denied a teaching position in Bloomington's public school system, a result of one of the prevailing prejudices of the day. The reason? She had become pregnant. From today's enlightened vantage point, Miller is bewildered by her apparent willingness to acquiesce to the "No Pregnant Need Apply" restriction that barred her from teaching in Monroe County. "We just accepted it as the way of the world. We are all prisoners of the times in which we live," she says unapologetically. "But sometimes we're able to break out." Miller's breakout point was yet to come, however.

Eventually finding clerical work in the IU purchasing office, Miller soon learned the value of personal connections. Because there were so many PHTs, and with teaching being one of the few job choices available for "the little woman," positions within the public school system were in high demand. But her ever-more-visible pregnancy was not an obstacle when it came to teaching grown-ups, so she became a night school instructor in an adult education program. Miller struck up a friendship with the night school program director, who helped her secure a prized junior high school teaching assignment once the baby was born.

In addition to her other obligations, Miller pursued her educational goals by studying for a master's degree in guidance and counseling. The rigors of a new baby, a full-time junior high teaching job, and the adult education classes—all the while supporting her law school spouse—might have overwhelmed a less stalwart scrambler. Every bit as goal-oriented as her husband, Miller weathered this intense crucible and emerged strengthened and with an enhanced level of confidence in her own abilities.

When her husband graduated from law school, the Millers packed off to Fort Wayne to begin their new life. The move eventually would bring about the dramatic changes that began when Miller rang Baekgaard's bell that fateful summer day, but positive change was a value she already had come to cherish.

A commitment to positive change has been a consistent hallmark of Miller's life and of her life's work as she has continued to rally against "gelification"—a word she coined to describe what happens when people become set in their ways. "We need to stay liquid, especially in today's rapidly changing world," she explains.

Miller enjoyed the challenges of her new life as a business owner, striving to be innovative and flexible as she and Baekgaard built the Vera Bradley organization. The result was the company's phenomenal success in bringing a formerly haute couture item to a mass market. In the process they learned that making women's purses from fabric instead of more durable material, such as leather, had some particular advantages: Women found the softer contours of the Vera Bradley bag to be more "cuddly" and comfortable. Even better, well-worn cloth purses typically don't last as long as leather bags, resulting in more rapid replacement sales. Also, unlike leather bags, most Vera Bradley products are machine washable.

Turning a potential negative into a positive is characteristic of Miller and Baekgaard's business style. The patterned bags are very distinctive, so the company accelerates the product replacement cycle by designing original fabric patterns on a seasonal basis. This tactic caters to their loyal customers' desire to own—and show off—the latest and greatest Vera Bradley bag.

The partners quickly understood the importance of carefully setting the proper price point in driving sales of their new "American-bred" line of fabric bags. Recalling how the original French provincial purses that inspired them were priced to the carriage trade, Miller and Baekgaard were determined to place their products within the budget range of the upscale modern American woman. At the same time, Vera Bradley products never were positioned in the "discount" or "knock-off" category. "Our purses are not cheap, but they're not expensive either. They're priced just right," Miller proclaims. Over the years, she says, the Vera Bradley brand has burnished its reputation as a "premium" quality line while avoiding the overpriced aura of high fashion.

Eschewing the "cookie cutter" school of merchandising, the company rarely offers its wares in mass-market department stores, preferring the more personalized environment of finer gift shops and boutiques. While much of the custom fabric is today manufactured overseas, all of the company's prized patterns are designed in-house under Baekgaard's watchful direction.

Today, the product line encompasses a host of fashionable accessories including duffels, totes, clutch bags—all featuring the distinctive quilted construction and unique trim. Its most recent offering: home furnishings, dubbed "The Vera Bradley Lifestyle." The company also is pursuing a younger demographic: the junior high, high school, and college markets. Attracted to a "fun" patterned accessory, young women have been drawn to the Vera Bradley brand in increasing numbers, prompting the company to open its first corporate-owned store at San Francisco Center in 2007. The line is sold at more than 3,600 stores nationwide, but the San Francisco store is the first of eight retail venues fully owned by the privately held corporation.

As Vera Bradley Designs has grown, so has Miller's commitment to the values she cherishes. High among those is her devotion to her alma mater, Indiana University. A longtime alumna and supporter, Miller was named to the IU Foundation board of directors in 2002. In that role, she became acquainted with Jim Morris, then president of the IU Board of Trustees. In early 2004, Miller received a fateful phone call from Morris: "Pat, I'd like you to drive to Indianapolis to meet a friend of mine," he said, somewhat mysteriously. Then he revealed the mystery man to be Mitch Daniels, who was seeking the Republican nomination for Indiana governor.

That March, Miller and the candidate enjoyed a get-acquainted luncheon, after which she confessed: "I like you. I really do." Daniels explained his need for self-made entrepreneurs such as Miller to help guide his campaign and, later, his administration and the state, back to economic health. She was impressed with his sincerity, intellect, and clear, down-to-earth sensibilities. The feeling evidently was mutual. Within two months, Daniels asked Miller to serve on the campaign and, if that went well, to become the state's first secretary of commerce.

As he did with each of his other cabinet appointees, candidate Daniels asked Miller to commit to at least two years of service. The decision was a wrenching one. To say "yes" meant leaving the management burden of Vera Bradley on Baekgaard's shoulders for even longer. Miller would need to spend the rest of 2004 on the road and then, if successful, would move to Indianapolis. Was it worth it? Could her potential accomplishments possibly outweigh the cost to her business and to her family? Miller grappled with these and other concerns as Daniels awaited her reply. In the end, she opted to devote herself to serving the state that had provided her, her family, and her business with such an incredible array of opportunities.

In May 2004, at the Vera Bradley headquarters in Fort Wayne, Daniels announced Miller as his choice to serve as secretary of commerce. They then traveled to Bedford, where Daniels announced his choice of Becky Skillman as his running mate. Although she had no prior political experience, Miller jumped into the campaign with a passion that impressed everyone. Weekends found her parading through small towns and Hoosier hamlets as part of the candidate's entourage, toting a banner that bore the somewhat puzzling moniker, "Secretary of Commerce Designee." More than one baffled voter would approach Miller at each campaign stop and ask: "What is that supposed to mean?" And she would patiently explain—over and over again. Miller made countless appearances at auto plants, trade associations, chamber of commerce meetings, and church picnics. At each one, she would extol the American dream, as corny as that may sound. Audiences were genuinely moved by her straightforward sincerity and her inspiring story of success. Without relying upon notes or teleprompters, Miller's stump speech was as consistent as it was compelling:

"I'm Pat Miller from Fort Wayne, and twenty-two years ago my partner and I started a women's handbag company with $500 and a notion that anything is possible if you are willing to work hard. Today, Vera Bradley Designs is a global company, selling over a million purses a year. Mitch Daniels has asked me to work just as hard to rebuild our state's economy as I did building Vera Bradley. With your help, that's exactly what I intend to do." She would soon have her chance as the voters of Indiana swept Daniels into office in November 2004.

Miller recalls her first cabinet meeting with wistful fondness. As she took her seat in the governor's meeting room and looked about the perimeter of the table, it struck her: There she was—the grocery girl from Farmington—seated directly to the governor's right, in the company of the state's top political, educational, and business leaders. "What on earth am I doing here?" she thought to herself. "I'm really in some rare air now."

Daniels quickly introduced Skillman, his lieutenant governor, and then, to underscore the priority he placed on economic development, called on Miller to spell out her goals for revitalizing the state's languishing commercial and industrial growth. She ditched her self-doubt and outlined a program of incentives and aggressive outreach that would, in short order, attract new growth to the state from all quarters of the globe.

Over the ensuing year, Miller helped attract major new industry to the state. This quest took her to Japan, where she found herself seated across the table from the CEO of the world's largest automaker, trying to sell him on the advantages of setting up shop in Indiana. In preparing for her negotiations with Toyota Motor Corporation, Miller studied the company's history and was amazed to learn of a common thread that ran between the automaker and her own company. Toyota was founded in 1937 as an offshoot of the Toyoda Automatic Loom Works. While the Toyota Group is today best known for its cars, it still produces fully computerized automatic looms and sewing machines. It is quite likely that Toyota looms are today used to create the very fabrics used by Vera Bradley Designs to manufacture its products.

The rest of Miller's high-performance tenure was marked by similar encounters, at home and abroad, that helped to lay the groundwork for what has been labeled an Indiana economic renaissance.

After one year in office—and nearly two years away from her business—Miller informed the governor that it was time for her to return to Fort Wayne. In December 2005, she turned over the reins to Indianapolis businessman Michael S. Maurer, who had been serving as president of the Indiana Economic Development Corporation.

But would Miller ever again enter the realm of public service if called upon to do so? If the governor, or the party, knocked upon her door, would she heed the call? What about her own political ambitions? "I have only the greatest admiration for Governor Daniels," she says unequivocally, "and I intend to continue giving him my full support. As for my own political plans, I've got plenty to keep me busy right here at Vera Bradley."

Today, Miller sits at the hub of an ever-evolving business, one of

Indiana's best-known homegrown success stories. Among that hub's most important spokes is the Vera Bradley Foundation. Established in 1998 after a friend of both Miller and Baekgaard's lost a valiant battle with breast cancer, the foundation has raised more than $6 million via the Vera Bradley Golf Classic and other fundraising initiatives. The money is directed toward research in the effort to eradicate breast cancer. Under Miller's guidance, the foundation has funded two major endowments to the IU School of Medicine. The gifts support the Vera Bradley Chair in Oncology and the Vera Bradley Center for Breast Cancer Research. Miller speaks with unabashed enthusiasm when she discusses the foundation's activities.

"Dr. Linda Malkas," she explains, referring to the current holder of the Vera Bradley chair, "and her team are working on a new biomarker system that can disclose genetic information that will bring about earlier breast cancer detection. It's really exciting, cutting-edge work."

The foundation boasts that every dollar raised goes directly into research, with none of it being siphoned off to pay for staff and salaries. It is governed by a volunteer board, and the salary of its development director is underwritten by Vera Bradley. The business further provides support by directing to the foundation a portion of the revenue generated by a selected Vera Bradley pattern.

The one enduring quality that defines and distinguishes Miller is her keen sense of corporate citizenship. Through word and deed, she has repeatedly demonstrated her understanding that in business, some priorities go well beyond producing a profit. Through her example, she has inspired young women across Indiana and beyond to pursue their most ambitious dreams. Through her stint in state government, she has shown the value of applying the lessons of private enterprise to the realm of public service. And through her work on behalf of the fight against breast cancer, Miller has shown how compassion and commitment to a cause can play a vital and affirming role in today's business environment.

Be it civic leader, business maven, charitable champion, or whatever "new bag" she gets into, Patricia Miller stands today as one of Indiana's brightest shining stars.

Michael S. Maurer served as Secretary of Commerce under Governor
Mitch Daniels. He is a regular columnist for the *Indianapolis Business
Journal* and an irregular contributor to the *New York Times* crossword
puzzle. He is author of *Water Colors: The Photographs of Michael S.
Maurer*, a book of his underwater macro photography. He lives in
Carmel, Indiana, with his wife, Janie. The Maurers have three children
and seven grandchildren.